Junior Jetsetters Guide to Toronto
First edition October 2007
ISBN-13: 978-0-9784601-0-5

Published by Junior Jetsetters Inc.
text © Junior Jetsetters Inc. 2007 and authors as indicated
photographs © photographers as indicated
character drawing © Junior Jetsetters Inc. 2007
illustrations © Junior Jetsetters Inc. 2007

Front cover photograph: Pedro F Marcelino
Front cover Junior Jetsetters logo: Tapan Gandhi

Printed by Webcom Inc.
Printed and bound in Canada.

JUNIOR JETSETTERS
GUIDE TO
TORONTO

TEXT
Slawko Waschuk
Pedro F Marcelino

CHARACTERS
Tapan Gandhi

ILLUSTRATIONS
Rob Bursey

TORONTO

This book is organized in three parts: an introductio. (Welcome to Toronto), attractions and activities i. and around Toronto, and finally a reference sectio. with information for your parents. Use the attractio. numbers and colour code to quickly find any locatior

PAGE 10
Welcome to Toronto

TORONTO ATTRACTIONS

ACTIVITIES

OUT OF TOWN

N

Baselands

Spine Road

Outer
Harbour
Marina

Outer Harbour

Embayment D

Cell 1
Wetland

Bird Research Station

Peninsula D

Embayment C

Cell 2

Peninsula C

Embayment B

Pedestrian
Bridge

Peninsula B

Triangle
Pond

Cell 3

Endikement

Embayment A

East Cove

Peninsula A

Goldfish Pond

Toplands

Endikement Tip

Spine Road

Lighthouse Point

Toronto Island Park

LEGEND

🍴 Snack Bar   ■ Historic Plaque   👫 Washrooms

1. Island Paradise Restaurant
2. Lockers
3. Toronto Hong Kong Lions Club Pavilion
4. Island Information Booth
5. Island Outfitters Kiosk
6. First Aid/Lost Children/Lost Parent Station
7. Police Station
8. Lagoon Theatre
9. Centreville Amusement Park
10. Carousel Café
11. Far Enough Farm
12. Island Tram Tour Departure
13. Harbour Tours Kiosk
14. Amazing Maze
15. The Boat House – Boat Rentals
16. Island Bicycle Rental
17. Pier
18. Changerooms/Lockers
19. Wading Pool/Saturn Playground
20. Franklin Children's Garden
21. Island Public and Natural Science School
22. Island Filtration Plant
23. T.I.R. Ropes Challenge Course
24. Gibraltar Point Centre for the Arts
25. Gibraltar Point Lighthouse
26. Island Yacht Club
27. Babe Ruth's First Professional Home Run Plaque
28. Ned Hanlan Statue
29. Toronto Island Marina
30. St. Andrews by the Lake Church
31. Fire Station
32. Disc Golf Course
33. Shaw House Seniors Co-op
34. The Rectory Cafe and Island Information
35. Island Canoe Club
36. Ward Island Association Clubhouse
37. Queen City Yacht Club
38. Algonquin Island Association Clubhouse
39. Royal Canadian Yacht Club
40. Toronto Island Information Booth @ Pier 6

ISLAND INFORMATION: 416-397-BOAT (2628)   **VISIT ON-LINE: www.toronto.ca/parks**

🍁 TORONTO Parks, Forestry & Recreation

Toronto is the capital of the Province of Ontario and is the largest city in Canada. It covers 641 square kilometres (247 square miles), stretching 43 kilometres (27 miles) from east to west and 21 kilometres (13 miles) from north to south. The population of Toronto is 2.5 million people, making up 8% of Canada's total population. The Greater Toronto Area (GTA) has a population of well over 5.55 million (18% of Canada's population). One-quarter of Canada's population is located within 160 kilometres (100 miles) of Toronto. It is the 5th largest city in North America, after Mexico City, New York, Los Angeles and Chicago, and it continues to grow.

The name Toronto comes from the Huron (also known as Wyandot) word for "fishing weir" (an ancient type of fish trap). The Huron are an Iroquoian First Nations people. Toronto is often pronounced Toronno (if you want to sound like you really belong, try calling it Tronno – the way it's pronounced by Torontonians). Toronto is located on the northern shore of Lake Ontario, not far from the Canadian-U.S. border at Niagara Falls and Buffalo, New York. Toronto is the economic capital of Canada and due to its international population, it continues to attract immigrants This has made it one of the world's most diverse cities.

Toronto versus the GTA

The current city of Toronto was formed in 1998 by the amalgamation (the fusion) of Toronto, Etobicoke, York, East York, North York and Scarborough. While visiting Toronto, you may hear the term GTA (Greater Toronto Area). The GTA now consists of the city of Toronto as well as the surrounding regional municipalities of Durham, Halton, Peel and York.

History

The first indigenous people (often called First Nations people) moved to the Toronto area almost 11,000 years ago. Europeans started to appear in the 17th century, with the French building small trading posts in the 18th century. The Toronto area was purchased from the Mississaugas (a tribe of First

Nations people) in 1787. Due to the threat of an American invasion, in 1793 John Graves Simcoe, then Lieutenant Governor of Upper Canada, established York, a military post and town, to improve the colony's defences. The village of Niagara, the provincial capital at the time, was subsequently moved to York. Over the next 20 years, York grew slowly. By 1815, as a capital, it had attracted banks and schools and in 1834, it was incorporated as the City of Toronto. By 1853, Toronto was a modern city, with residential and commercial neighbourhoods, gas lighting, piped water, and the beginnings of a rail system. After Confederation in 1867 (when Canada was formed), industrialization helped expand and shape the city, which grew quickly and reached 208,000 residents by 1901. In 1904, the Great Toronto Fire destroyed a large downtown section (after which the fire department was extended). The city was quickly rebuilt and soon became Canada's most important economic and cultural centre. By 1941, the population had reached 667,000 residents. Numerous waves of immigration after 1945 helped Toronto become one of the most multicultural cities in the World.

Today, almost half the population was born outside Canada. Toronto continues to grow, with a strong economy, rich culture and good working and living conditions. It is often pointed out as one of the best cities in the world to live in.

Government of Canada

Canada is the second largest country in the world. The word Canada comes from an Iroquoian word meaning "village". Ottawa is the capital and is, therefore, the centre of government for Canada.

Canada is a Commonwealth country with close ties to the United Kingdom. It is now a sovereign state that was once a British colony. This history has helped the two countries maintain excellent relations. The Queen has, to date, visited Canada 21 times. Although Canada is no longer a colony, it is a parliamentary democracy and a constitutional monarchy with Elizabeth II, Queen of Canada, as the Head of State. The Governor General is The Queen's representative in Canada and is responsible for carrying out Her Majesty's duties on a daily basis. Some of the Governor General's responsibilities include: giving Royal Assent to bills passed by the government, reading the Speech from the Throne, opening and ending sessions of Parliament and dissolving Parliament for an election. The Governor General is also the Commander-in-Chief. There is a clear distinction between the Head of State and the Head of Government. The Head of Government is the Prime Minister.

Canada's Parliament consists of the Queen (or Crown), represented by the Governor General, the Senate and the House of Commons. Voters elect members of the House of Commons, known as Members of Parliament. The Governor General, based on the Prime Minister's recommendation, appoints senators to the Senate. The House of Commons is responsible for making laws. Bills are drafted and may be passed by the House, at which time they are sent to the Senate. The Senate can amend or reject any bill. Once the bill has passed the Senate, the Governor General can give Royal Assent, making the bill a law (also known as an Act). Federal Acts begin with "Her Majesty, by and with the advice and consent of the Senate and the House of Commons, enacts as follows:".

Government of Ontario

As the capital of Ontario, Toronto is the seat of government for Canada's largest and most populated province. Ontario accounts for 39% of Canada's entire population. Ontario's government is called the Legislative Assembly of Ontario and is located in Queen's Park. Ontario uses a constitutional monarchy system of government. Queen Elizabeth II, as the reigning Queen of Canada has a representative in Ontario, known as the Lieutenant Governor of Ontario, who is appointed by the Governor General. The Lieutenant Governor gives Royal Assent to all bills passed in Ontario, making them law.

Bills are introduced in the Legislative Assembly. The bill is given several readings in the Assembly, allowing for review by all members, debate and amendments. When the bill is given Royal Assent by the Lieutenant Governor, it becomes an Act. There is no senate. Provincial Acts begin with "Her Majesty, by and with the advice and consent of the Legislative Assembly of the Province of Ontario, enacts as follows:".

Government of Toronto

The City of Toronto is governed by City Council with one elected mayor and many elected city councillors. Each councillor represents a city ward (an electoral district). City Council makes decisions regarding city policy, priorities and levels of service. Council manages different departments through numerous Committees. Committee meetings present an opportunity for citizens to make their views known. Toronto is Canada's sixth largest government. The City was given new powers on January 1, 2007 to allow the government to make policies to achieve "prosperity, opportunity and livability". The government can now pass by-laws to promote the well-being of the City and its people, to create new ways to raise money, to be more involved in planning decisions and how land is developed and to make agreements with other governments without getting permission from the Government of Ontario.

Neighbourhoods

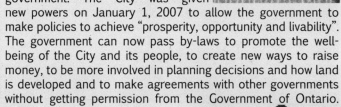

Toronto is made up of many distinct neighbourhoods, some of which are identified by street signs. Architectural styles may also vary from neighbourhood to neighbourhood. Landmark neighbourhoods include: Queen's Quay, Harbourfront, Queen Street West, Fashion District, Financial District, St. Lawrence, Portugal Village, Chinatown, Regent Park, Little Italy, Cabbagetown, Seaton Village, The Annex, Yorkville, Summerhill, Rosedale, Roncesvalles Village, The Beach, Greektown, Bloor West Village, High Park, Kensington Market, Little India, Riverdale, Leslieville, Mimico, New Toronto, Weston, Leaside, Long Branch, Swansea, Forest Hill, and many more.

PATH

Toronto's downtown has an underground walkway that links shopping, services and entertainment. PATH allows you to **13** reach your downtown destination easily without worrying about the winter weather outside. It connects to five subway stations, twenty parking garages, six hotels, two department stores, Union Station and more than 50 buildings/office towers. There are approximately 1,200 shops and services in PATH. It also connects to some of Toronto's major attractions (included in the Junior Jetsetters Guide to Toronto) such as: the Hockey Hall of Fame, Roy Thomson Hall, Air Canada Centre, Rogers Centre, the CN Tower and City Hall. According to Guinness World Records, PATH is the largest underground shopping complex in the world with 27 kilometres (16 miles) of shopping arcades. It has 371,600 square metres (4 million square feet) of retail space. Note: Each letter in PATH is a different colour, each representing a direction. The P is red and represents south. The orange A directs pedestrians to the west, while the blue T directs them to the north. The H is yellow and points to the east. Trying out this true underground city should be on your must-do list!

High Park

Toronto's High Park is one of the most significant natural sites in the city. It is located west of the downtown area and spans 161 hectares (399 acres). Over one-third of the park remains in a natural state. It is home to many species of birds, fish and animals as well as rare plant species. The park offers the opportunity for many activities. The Jamie Bell Adventure Playground is intended as a family meeting place. Grenadier Pond is located in the southern part of the park and is home to many species of birds and marsh wildlife. To tour the park, hop on the trackless train, which offers a 25-minute scenic ride. There is also a zoo with bison, llamas, peacocks, deer, cattle and sheep. Cycling is allowed only on paved roads. Walking trails throughout the park are marked and the High Park Citizen's Advisory Committee offers walking tours. In the winter, why not enjoy a day of cross-country skiing? Additionally, tennis courts, an outdoor swimming pool, an outdoor artificial ice rink and picnic areas are available for public use.

People

Toronto is one of the most multicultural cities in the world, with Canadian, English, Scottish, Irish, Chinese, Italian, East Indian, French, German, Portuguese, Polish, Jewish, Jamaican, Filipino, Ukrainian, Dutch, Greek, Spanish, Russian, Hungarian, Sri Lankan, Vietnamese, Welsh, Korean, Pakistani, Iranian, West Indian, Guyanese and aboriginal people as the largest groups. 43% of Toronto's population consider themselves to be part of a visible minority and 49% of Toronto's population was born outside of Canada. Toronto has 79 ethnic publications.

Famous People

Actors: Christopher Plummer, John Candy, Catherine O'Hara, Rick Moranis, Howie Mandel, Jim Carrey, Mike Myers, Keanu Reeves, Kiefer Sutherland, Eric McCormack, Sarah Polley
Artists: Joe Shuster (creator of "Superman"), Frank Gehry (architect)
Musicians/Bands: Glenn Gould (pianist), Neil Young (singer), SNOW (rapper), Amanda Marshall (singer), Barenaked Ladies (band)

Language

Although Canada is officially bilingual (English and French), the main language spoken in Toronto is English. French is not widely spoken or understood in the city. Government services and information are available in English and French. However, because of the multicultural nature of the city, you will undoubtedly hear other languages being spoken every day, as over 100 languages and dialects are spoken here. The most common are Italian, Mandarin, Cantonese, Portuguese, Punjabi, Spanish, Polish, Tagalog (Philippines), Tamil, French, Urdu, Greek, Russian, Ukrainian and Arabic.

Getting here

BY AIR – There are two airports in Toronto. Lester B. Pearson International Airport is located just west of the city and Toronto City Centre Airport is located on the western tip of the Toronto Islands. **BY BUS** – The Bus Terminal is located at 610 Bay Street. Most major routes (serving Ontario, Canada, and the U.S.) come together in Toronto. **BY TRAIN** – VIA Rail provides train service throughout Canada and connects to Amtrak in Niagara Falls, New York. Trains arrive at Union Station, located on Front Street between Bay and University and on the subway line. **BY CAR** – Several major highways bypass Toronto. Hwy 401 enters the city from the east and west. The Gardiner Expressway/Queen Elizabeth Way (QEW) enters the city from the west. Hwy 400 enters from the north and connects with Hwy 401. **BY BOAT** – Docking facilities exist for boaters who wish to arrive to Toronto by water. Information can be obtained from the Toronto Port Authority.

Getting around by public transportation

TTC – The Toronto Transit Commission (TTC) is the public transportation system in Toronto. It consists of subways, light rail trains, buses and streetcars, which link together to allow travellers to get around Toronto. (Note: Streetcars can be chartered for private tours/trips. 65 people can enjoy an individually-designed route for just under $800 for three hours.). **GTA** – Mississauga Transit, Brampton Transit, Viva, Durham Region Transit and GO Transit outside of Toronto connect to the TTC. **TAXIS** – Several taxi companies service Toronto and most use distinctive colours. Taxis are an easy way to get from place to place while visiting the city. **BICYCLING** – Toronto is becoming a more bicycle friendly city. Many streets have exclusive bicycle lanes and there are plans for a comprehensive bikeway network. Currently there are 187 kilometres (116 miles) of bike paths. Always remember to wear a helmet. Not only does it make sense, but it's the law in Ontario that all cyclists under 18 wear an approved bicycle helmet when riding a bike. **BOAT** – Ferries connect the city to the Toronto Islands. The ferry terminal is located at Bay Street and Queen's Quay. The schedule changes depending on the season. Be careful you don't miss the last boat back!

Tourist Information

Tourism Toronto: 1-800-499-2514 (toll free) or 416-203-2600 (also hotel reservations). See www.torontotourism.com.

InfoTOgo

InfoTOgo pillars, located throughout Toronto, display a map specifically designed for each area. Maps include places of interest, historic locations, public transit and area descriptions. Pocket-sized maps are available from the map dispensers, which require a $2 coin (toonie).

City Pass

One reduced price for 6 attractions: CN Tower, Casa Loma, Hockey Hall of Fame, Ontario Science Centre, ROM and Zoo. The pass also helps you avoid ticket lines at most attractions. Available for adults/children at these attractions.

Disabled

Most public facilities now offer disabled access. TTC provides Wheel-Trans for those using wheelchairs (book in advance).

Climate & Weather

Because of its southern location and closeness to Lake Ontario, Toronto has a moderate climate. Summers are warm and humid; winters are generally cold. Spring, summer, fall and winter are distinct seasons in the city. Canada is famous for its 'Indian summer' in early Fall, when trees change colours. Watch out for green, brown, golden, yellow, orange, red and burgundy maple leaves (Canada's national symbol)! Visit Humber Bay Park, High Park, Centennial Park or the Don Valley to watch the colour show. Tip: look for a bridge over the Don Valley, and watch from above. If you're visiting in the winter, make sure to bring a "tuque" (a knitted hat) and mitts. It can get very cold in Toronto!

Time

Eastern Time Zone (EST, or GMT-5), same as New York City.

Business Hours

Shops: usually 10am-6pm (check specific times). Government offices: usually 8:30am-4:30pm. Banks: 9am-5pm

Holidays

Public holidays in Toronto are New Year's Day (January 1), Good Friday (Friday before Easter Sunday), Victoria Day (Monday on or before May 24), Canada Day (July 1), Simcoe Day (first Monday in August), Labour Day (first Monday in September), Thanksgiving (second Monday in October), Christmas Day (December 25) and Boxing Day (December 26). Most stores, all government offices, postal services, and banks are closed on these holidays. Tourist attractions are usually open

Money

The currency in Canada is the Canadian dollar ($). A dollar is made up of 100 cents (¢). Coins are: penny (1 cent), nickel (5 cents), dime (10 cents), quarter (25 cents), loonie (1 dollar) and toonie/twoonie (2 dollars). The loonie got its name from the loon (duck) on one of the sides of the coin. Notes come in denominations of $5, $10, $20, $50 and $100 (there are also $1,000 notes, but you won't easily spot one!).

Telephones

Toronto has two area codes, 416 and 647. The GTA's area codes are 905 and 289. To make a call, you must dial the area code followed by the seven-digit phone number. Some, but not all, 905 and 289 numbers are long distance from Toronto and, therefore, require you to dial 1-905 or 1-289. Toll-free numbers (starting with 1-800, 1-888, 1-877, 1-866) are free of charge from Toronto. Bell Canada pay phones accept credit cards, phone cards and 25¢ quarters (no change given!). Cards are available in convenience stores, automatic dispensers and Bell outlets around Toronto.

Emergency services

In Canada, police, the fire department and ambulance services are centralized in one number: 911 (free from any pay phone).

Postal Services

Canada Post offices are rare. Visit www.canadapost.ca for store
locations and Canada Post representatives.   Stamps are widely
available in shops or at postal outlets/counters around the city. **19**

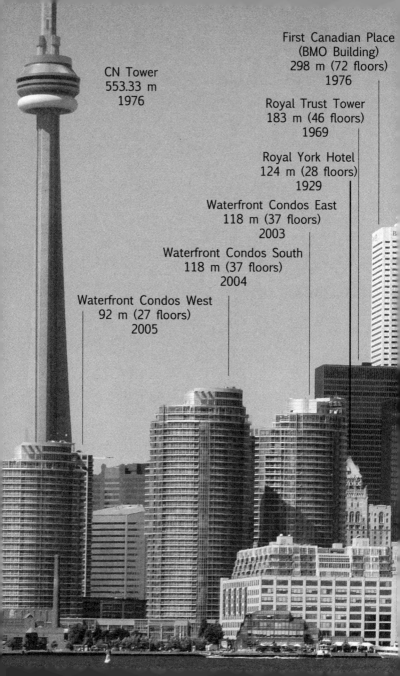

First Canadian Place
(BMO Building)
298 m (72 floors)
1976

CN Tower
553.33 m
1976

Royal Trust Tower
183 m (46 floors)
1969

Royal York Hotel
124 m (28 floors)
1929

Waterfront Condos East
118 m (37 floors)
2003

Waterfront Condos South
118 m (37 floors)
2004

Waterfront Condos West
92 m (27 floors)
2005

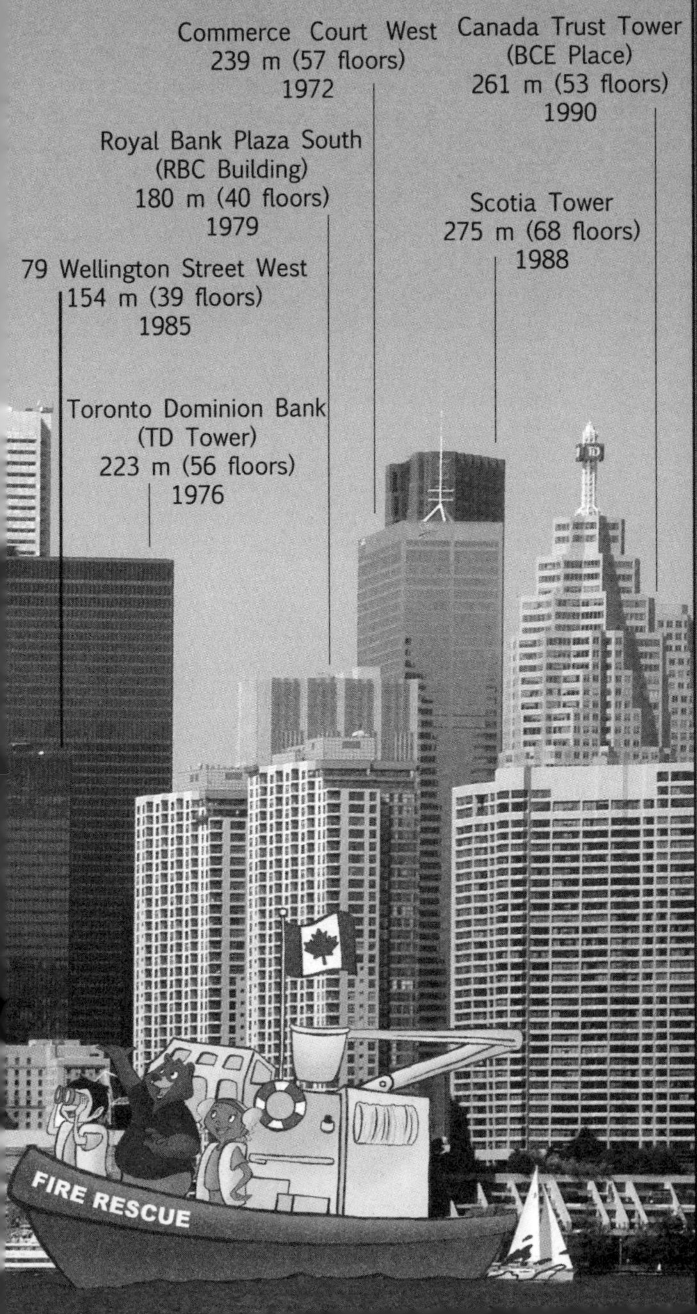

Commerce Court West
239 m (57 floors)
1972

Canada Trust Tower
(BCE Place)
261 m (53 floors)
1990

Royal Bank Plaza South
(RBC Building)
180 m (40 floors)
1979

Scotia Tower
275 m (68 floors)
1988

79 Wellington Street West
154 m (39 floors)
1985

Toronto Dominion Bank
(TD Tower)
223 m (56 floors)
1976

FIRE RESCUE

The CN Tower, Canada's most recognizable icon, stands at a height of 553.33 metres (1,815 feet, 5 inches). It has held several world records, including the World's Tallest Free-standing Structure, the World's Tallest Building and the World's Tallest Tower. It was the World's Tallest Building and Free-standing Structure for over 30 years. It was finally surpassed by the Burj Dubai in the United Arab Emirates on September 13, 2007 (32 years, 5 months and 11 days after being finished). CN Tower also hosts the World's Highest Wine Cellar. Although it was initially designed as a telecommunications structure, the Tower also offers breath-taking views of Toronto and the surrounding area. On a clear day you can see as far as Niagara Falls! Your high-altitude experience begins with a quick elevator ride to the main pod. The elevator travels at 22 km/hour (15 miles/hour), reaching the Look Out Level in 58 seconds. There are three observation levels: the Look Out Level is 346 metres (1,136 feet) above ground level; the Glass Floor, at 342 metres (1,122 feet), allows you to look straight down below your feet; the Sky Pod at 447 metres (1,465 feet). The main pod also houses two restaurants, a gift shop, and the World's Highest Mailbox! At the base of the Tower, the Maple Leaf Cinema shows the film The Height of Excellence, documenting the construction of the CN Tower. Next door, don't miss the motion theatre ride, a unique flight simulation experience that you won't soon forget. There is also an Arcade featuring the latest in interactive games.

Time lapse

10 tallest in the world:

1. Burj Dubai, 555 m (final: 800)
   DUBAI, UNITED ARAB EMIRATES
2. CN Tower, 553.33 m
   TORONTO, CANADA
3. Ostankino Tower, 540 m
   MOSCOW, RUSSIA
4. Taipei 101, 508 m
   TAIPEI, TAIWAN
5. Oriental Pearl Tower, 468 m
   SHANGHAI, CHINA
6. Petronas Towers, 452 m
   KUALA LUMPUR, MALAYSIA
7. Sears Tower, 442 m
   CHICAGO, USA
8. Milad Tower, 435 m
   TEHRAN, IRAN
9. Kuala Lumpur Tower, 421 m
   KUALA LUMPUR, MALAYSIA
10. Jin Mao Building, 421 m
    SHANGHAI, CHINA

Get this...

lightning strikes the CN Tower on average 75 times per year ● the Tower can withstand an earthquake of 8.5 on the Richter scale ● the Glass Floor can withstand the weight of 14 large hippos! ● the main stairwell has 1,776 steps ● the 360 Restaurant revolves once every 72 minutes ● a time capsule was sealed in the tower in 1976, and is to be opened in 2076 ● approximately 2 million visitors come each year ● 1,537 workers worked 24 hours a day, five days a week, for 40 months to complete the Tower

Get this...

the name "house on the hill" or Casa Loma was given to the property by its previous owner ● Sir Henry lived in the castle for less than 10 years ● the 244 metre (800 foot) tunnel lies 5.5 metres (18 feet) below the ground ● a secret passage connects the wine cellar directly to Sir Henry's study ● the castle has 22 fireplaces ● the foundations are set 14 metres (45 feet) deep

If you think you recognize the Castle, you are right! Over the years it has been used in many movies. They include: X-Men, The Pacifier, The Tuxedo, Johnny Mnemonic, Cocktail, Maximum Risk

Casa Loma was the dream castle of Sir Henry Pellatt. In 1911, he hired Canadian architect E.J. Lennox (who also designed Old City Hall) to build his "house on the hill". It took 300 men almost three years to build and cost $3.5 million. Sir Henry's financial situation changed and he was unable to complete the castle. Many rooms and areas were left unfinished. He was forced to auction many of his possessions for a fraction of their value and to leave his home in 1924. Today, it is one of Toronto's top attractions. Take the secret passage on the left in the Study up to the second floor. Climb the 144 stairs to the top of the Scottish Tower. Head over to the Stables through the 800 foot-long underground tunnel.

The Toronto Eaton Centre is one of Canada's best-known shopping destinations with over 285 shops and services. It attracts millions of tourists from around the world, making it one of the city's top destinations. Three office towers, each 300 feet tall, are connected to the centre. The Eaton Centre is located at the busy Queen and Yonge intersection. Yonge Street is often considered to be Toronto's main street and is home to many Toronto attractions, including Dundas Square, the Hockey Hall of Fame and several theatres. Yonge Street starts at Lake Ontario and continues all the way to Rainy River, 1,896 kilometres away, making it the world's longest street! Yonge-Dundas Square, located across the street from the Eaton Centre, is a central meeting point and is used as an event venue with community celebrations, theatrical performances, concerts and promotions.

Yonge Street

Get this...

the Toronto Eaton Centre was modeled after the Galleria Vittorio Emanuele in Milan, Italy ● even after the Eaton's chain went bankrupt in 1999 and was bought by Sears, the Centre kept its original name ● don't miss out on some delicacies in the area - including sushi, a Toronto favourite, and the best hot dogs in the city! ● behind the Centre, Trinity Square is a well-kept secret oasis

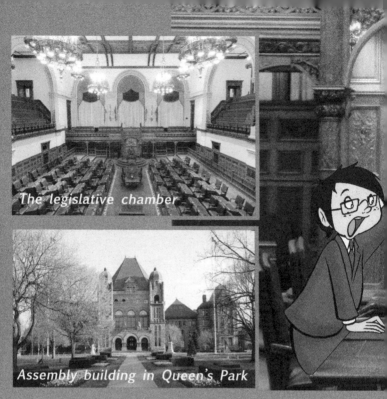

The legislative chamber

Assembly building in Queen's Park

The first inhabitants of Ontario were the Algonquian and Iroquoian tribes. Europeans began exploring the area in the early 17th century when both French and British explorers set up trading posts and settlements. In 1791, The Canadas were formed – Upper Canada (now Ontario) and Lower Canada (now Québec). On July 1, 1867 the British North America Act established the Dominion of Canada with four provinces: Nova Scotia, New Brunswick, Québec and Ontario. Toronto also officially became Ontario's provincial capital. The Government of Ontario was established and was named the Legislative Assembly of Ontario. Construction of the Legislative Building in Queen's Park began in 1886 and took six years to complete. In 1909, a fire destroyed the west wing. It was rebuilt by 1912, using Italian marble instead of the wood used in the rest of the building. The centre of the building hosts the Legislative Chamber where Members of the Provincial Parliament pass laws for Ontario. The Speaker runs the meetings in the Chamber and makes sure all rules are followed. The Sergeant-at-Arms is responsible for security. He also places the Mace on the Table to start the session.

Speaker of the House

Sergeant-at-Arms

The Mace of Ontario

Get this...

Parliament can only sit if the Mace is placed on the Table of the House in the Chamber ● the original Mace was taken by the Americans during the War

of 1812. It was returned in 1934 and is displayed in the main lobby ● a dinosaur fossil is located in one of the marble columns in the west wing, but no one agrees if it's real! ● people often call the Legislative Building "Queen's Park", which is wrong - Queen's Park is the name of the park only ● Queen's Park black squirrels are the cheekiest in Toronto!

Nathan Phillips Square is a popular gathering place right in front of Toronto City Hall. It was named for Nathan Phillips, the Mayor from 1955 to 1962. The Square holds many events such as WinterCity (outdoor entertainment including music & theatre), Fresh Wednesdays (a farmers' market during the summer and early fall), Tasty Thursdays (restaurants feature select menu items in July and August), the Cavalcade of Lights (a holiday tradition of lights decorating the square and a giant Christmas Tree in November and December), the Toronto Outdoor Art Exhibition (in July) and the Toronto Jazz Festival (in June). The Square has several unique features. In front of the futuristic City Hall stands Henry Moore's Three-Way Piece No. 2 (often called The Archer). The Peace Garden honours Torontonians' commitment to world peace. The Freedom Arches over the pond are a favourite spot for hundreds of pigeons. Read the plaque to learn the significance of the arches. The Square is also home to Oscar Nemon's statue of Sir Winston Churchill, the former Prime Minister of Great Britain. City Hall was designed through a competition in 1957. The winning design became Toronto's fourth and current City Hall. It opened in September 1965. The central dome is the Council Chamber. The whole City is run from this room.

Old City Hall

Get yours here!

City Hall:

520 designs from 42 countries were submitted • it cost $31 million to build • the ceiling of the Council Chamber weighs over 2,000 tonnes!!! • the concrete cladding took 40 days to dry

Toronto flags

Get this...

a piece of the Berlin Wall lays flat at the base of the centre freedom arch on the south side ● one of the world's largest underground parking garages is located beneath the Square. There is space for 2,400 cars

The Art Gallery of Ontario has over 68,000 works in its collection, spanning from 100 AD to the present. It houses an extensive Canadian art collection – 40% of the collection follows the development of Canada's art heritage since pre-Confederation. It has a large Inuit (northern natives) art collection and one of the most significant African art collections in North America. It houses the world's largest public collection of works by Henry Moore, a British artist and sculptor, known for his large-scale abstract cast bronze and carved marble sculptures. See also the collection of European art, with works by artists like Rodin, Monet, Degas, Cezanne, van Gogh, Picasso. The AGO hosts many exhibitions. Notable past exhibits include works by Andy Warhol, Tom Thomson (see McMichael) and Yoko Ono. In 2004, the AGO began a redevelopment known as Transformation AGO, designed by Toronto-born star-architect Frank Gehry.

Get this...

it is the 8th largest art museum in North America • the transformation will cost $254 million and will increase the museum to 54,160 square metres (583,000 square feet) • the Grange, built in 1817 is the fourth oldest surviving building in Toronto

The Grange

Titanium cladding

7

The Royal Ontario Museum (ROM) opened to the public in 1914. The Museum grew and continued to expand, requiring new galleries and buildings. Today, it is Canada's largest museum of world cultures and natural history. Its collection includes about six million objects. In addition to the galleries, the ROM also conducts important scientific and academic research. The most recent museum expansion, opened in 2007, is the Michael Lee-Chin Crystal, the unmissable building designed by Daniel Libeskind. The Spirit House is the heart of the Crystal and opens from top to bottom. Bridges join galleries on either side. If you like to touch things, the CIBC Discovery Gallery is filled with touchable artifacts and real specimens from the past, from other countries and cultures and from around Toronto. The Keenan Family Gallery of Hands-on Biodiversity focuses on the relationships among all living things and also has many specimens that can be handled.

The 2 buildings

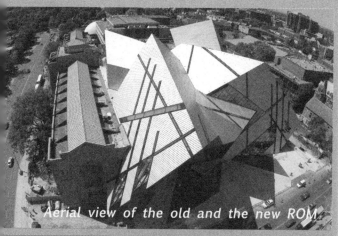

Aerial view of the old and the new ROM

Light show on the Crystal

Get this...

the initial idea for the Crystal was sketched on a napkin ● there are no right angles in the Crystal ● the Crystal is not attached to the original buildings except for the bridges, which have sliding connections to allow the Crystal to move slightly ● the ROM's most successful single exhibition was Egyptian Art in the Age of the Pyramids

The Ontario Science Centre is a science museum in Toronto. It opened in September 1969. The Centre was unique in that it offered a "hands on" approach to science. Interactive exhibits and live demonstrations allow you to experience science, not just see it. Have a question? Ask one of the hosts wearing white lab coats! They'll be able to help you or answer your questions. The Centre has several exhibition halls and areas. The Science Arcade contains puzzles, games, challenges and hands-on experiences to help you learn about science. Living Earth is another hands-on area that explores plants,

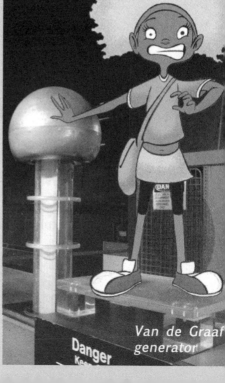

Van de Graaf generator

Danger

Get this...

over 39 million people have visited since the opening day ● more than 200,000 Canadian students visit every year ● it has been used in many movies and TV shows ● the Van de Graaff Generator is one of the most popular with visitors

animals and the environment. Learn all about yourself in the Human Body hall. The Sport hall shows you how science plays a role in sports. Or watch a movie in the very cool IMAX Dome - look out for the program at the entrance! The Centre also offers several week-long summer day camps. If you're in Toronto for a longer period, why not take a look? The Science Centre is often involved in research and visitors can sometimes participate. It's your chance to contribute to science as it is happening!

Living Earth

It's hands-on!

British garrison

Fort York was built by John Graves Simcoe in 1793. Simcoe, the Lieutenant Governor of Upper Canada (now Ontario), moved the capital here from Niagara, which was too close to the U.S. border. Soon a settlement named York started. With the British and Americans battling often, in 1807 the Fort's defences were strengthened by the addition of the west wall and circular battery. In 1812, the United States declared war on Canada and in April 1813, the US Army and Navy attacked the settlement. Armed with 12 cannons, 700 British, Canadians, and Mississauga and Ojibway natives defended York against 2,700 men on 14 ships with 85 cannons, but were eventually forced to retreat to the Fort and then further east. They blew up the Fort's gunpowder magazine, causing many casualties among the attackers, who then burned The Parliament Buildings and Government House (the Lieutenant Governor's residence) before leaving. They returned later and burned the remaining buildings. In 1814, the British had their turn and captured Washington and burned the U.S. Capitol and the president's residence. Fort York was rebuilt, and by 1814 it was able to hold off the Americans when they returned. By December, the war had ended. Canada had been successfully defended against the U.S. invasion. Over time, defences deteriorated, but when tension or war was expected (for example in 1837-41 and again in 1861-62) were strengthened. By 1880, the Fort was no longer used for defence. From 1880 to the 1930s, the Fort was used for training by the army.

Get this...

York was the original name of Toronto ● during the war of 1812 the U.S. president's house was painted white to cover the burns and since became known as The White House

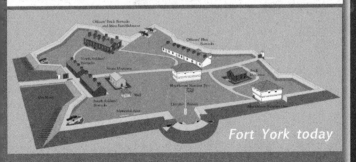

Fort York today

A visit to Toronto wouldn't be complete without a visit to the Harbourfront Centre, a cultural centre located on the waterfront. The PowerPlant is the contemporary art gallery at the Centre. You can't miss its smokestack (left over from the time it was a generating plant). The Toronto Music Garden (a few blocks west) offers music and dance programming during the summer. The Craft Studio lets you see professional artists creating ceramics, glass, metal and textiles. The Artists' Gardens are living displays created by designers, craftspeople and artists. They offer new ideas about gardening. The Nautical Centre offers sailing lessons. The Concert Stage is the site of a summer music program. It also offers camps, reading series, exhibition space, a visual arts centre and the Bounty craft shop.

Get this...

the Centre was part of a plan to bring city life back to the
waterfront – Harbourfront was the Canadian Government's
contribution and Ontario Place was Ontario's contribution
● Music Garden, designed by Yo Yo Ma and Julie Moir
Messervy, was inspired by Johann Sebastian Bach's First
Suite for Unaccompanied Cello ● the Concert Stage
offers free multicultural music every weekend from
Canada Day to Labour Day (July to early September)

The Toronto Islands (usually called "The Island") are a chain of islands across the harbour from downtown Toronto. The chain has three main islands and several smaller islets. This was not always the case. Up until 1858, these islands were a peninsula that extended from the mainland. A powerful storm broke up the peninsula into islands and separated them from the mainland. A channel was formed which was later deepened. The islands include the popular Centre Island, Olympic Island, Ward's Island and Algonquin Island and several others. It was once a popular summer retreat for Toronto's citizens and is now the permanent home for over 200 families. The Island is now considered a park with 230 hectares (570 acres). Several parks, an amusement park, marinas, yacht clubs and three beaches exist on The Island. Cars (except some service vehicles) are not permitted, making it perfect for cyclists, rollerbladers and walkers.   Ferries leave from downtown Toronto regularly and take

Get this...

over 1,225,000 people visit the islands every year ● Gibraltar Point Lighthouse is the oldest landmark in Toronto, built in 1808 ● the islands are the largest urban car-free community in North America ● baseball legend Babe Ruth hit his first professional home run at Hanlan's Point ● 262 houses are home to approximately 700 people who live on The Island

10-15 minutes to make the crossing. Rent a bicycle and explore The Island or try playing a round of golf on Canada's #1 disc golf course. Bring your fishing rod and catch a Bass, Bluegill or Pike in Lake Ontario! The Toronto Island Tram allows you to discover the history of The Island. Or why not rent a paddleboat or canoe and discover the many lagoons and waterways. Take a walk to the western side of The Island to the Gibraltar Point Lighthouse at Hanlan's Point. But be careful - rumour has it that it is now haunted by an old lighthouse keeper! The Toronto City Centre Airport is located on the western side of The Island, directly across from the mainland. A small ferry takes flyers across the Western Channel to the airport. According to Guinness World Records, it is the world's shortest scheduled ferry run.

Roller coaster

Located on Centre Island, Centreville is a family amusement park that has been operating for over 40 years. The park contains over 30 rides and attractions and is situated in over 230 hectares (570 acres) of parkland. It is just a 15-minute ferry ride away from downtown Toronto.

Hop on the Centreville Train that takes you all around the park. Or get an aerial view from the Sky Ride. This ride takes you over the park, Far Enough Farm and some of the water ways, and it offers you unique views of the Island and Toronto's downtown area and impressive skyline. Get your camera ready, as you will have only 10 seconds for your great skyline shots! Play a round of golf at the miniature golf course, or try driving Centreville's antique

Get this...

the Centreville Train has carried over 6 million passengers ● the Antique Carousel has over 52 animals, including horses, rabbits, cats, pigs, ostriches, a lion, tiger, giraffe, reindeer and zebra!

Park Rides

Bumper Boat Ride ● Motor Boat Ride ● Log Flume Ride ● Scrambler Ride ● Toronto Island Monster Coaster ● Miniature Golf Course ● Haunted Barrel Works ● Ferris Wheel ● Swan Ride ● Fire Engine Ride ● Sky Ride ● Bumble Bee Ride

Centreville train

cars. Go round and round on the Antique Carousel, get wet on the Saurgreen Lumber Co. Flume Ride, enjoy the views from the Windmill Ferris Wheel or take a spin on the Fire Engine Ride. For a more natural and tranquil experience, you can ride a pony near Far Enough Farm (but they leave The Island by the end of the season). If you're hungry, grab a Funnel Cake or a Beaver Tail!

Get this...

millions of cubic metres of concrete, earth fill and dredged sand have been used ● park is over 500 hectares (1,235 acres) ● site was not originally created as a park – it was built to allow for increased port facilities to accommodate more boats ● largest known colony of black-crowned night herons in Canada ● the park is a globally recognized Important Bird Area for colonial waterbirds and migrant songbirds ● snakes are the most common reptiles in the park

Tommy Thompson Park is located on a man-made peninsula, often called Leslie Street Spit, extending 5 km into Lake Ontario. Construction started in the 1950s and continued until recently. The peninsula grew from controlled lakefill from development sites in Toronto. Present lakefilling is meant to secure the existing shoreline. Over the years, wetlands, meadows and forests have been created by the Toronto Region and Conservation Authority and have matured enough to now provide a home to many endangered and rare species who nest in this area. To date, over 314 bird species have been seen, including gulls, terns, herons and cormorants. You may also see animals such as woodchucks, muskrats, beavers, raccoons, rabbits, red foxes and even coyotes! Eastern garter snakes, northern brown snakes, midland painted turtles, snapping turtles and American toads also live in the park. This urban wilderness is an ideal place for riding your bicycle, roller-blading, walking or bird watching. Late summer and early fall is a good time to see hundreds of monarch butterflies as they wait to migrate south.

Leslie Spit aerial view in 2005

Sunset in Kew Beach

Watch house

Seagulls

Cool life at The Beach

The Beach has been attracting people since 1870 and is Toronto's first lakeside resort. This popular neighbourhood is located in the east end. Old bungalows, sandy beaches and a Boardwalk along Lake Ontario make the area feel like cottage country. Spend some time in one of the parks. Go shopping in one of over 350 fine stores. Enjoy some homemade ice cream in one of the sidewalk cafés. There are many things to do at the Beach: volleyball, swimming, kite flying, dog walking, bicycling, running and canoeing are just a few. Relax and listen to some music. Talented musicians often perform for crowds. In July, you can enjoy one of Toronto's favourite events, the Beaches International Jazz Festival.

Lively streets!

Get this...

the name of the area is controversial – the official name is The Beach, but many people call the area the Beaches ● this section of Queen Street was chosen as Ontario's best small-town Main Street ● the Boardwalk stretches 3.1 kilometres ● Woodbine Beach is North America's first Blue Flag beach – meaning that the water is consistently safe and clean and that it meets the highest standards

Scooter, the alpaca

Masai giraffe

Australian emu

Siberian tiger

Tree kangaroo

Western grey kangaroo

Golden lion tamarin

Get this...

the Zoo spends $1,000,000 per year on food ● orangutans like to snack on yogurt ● no two zebras have stripes that are exactly alike ● a jelly fish is 95% water ● a group of kangaroos is called a "mob" ● a lion's roar can be heard for up to 8 km (5 miles) ● an elephant trunk has about 40,000 muscles

Riverdale was Toronto's main zoo until 1973. Construction of the current zoo began in 1970 and it officially opened in 1974. At that time, the wild animals were moved from Riverdale. The Zoo is divided into four major pavilions and several indoor exhibits. The plants and animals are grouped according to where they are naturally found. There are six zoogeographic (animal distribution) regions: African Savanna, Americas, Australasia, Canadian Domain, Eurasia and Indo-Malaya. The Zoo also contains the Zellers Discovery Zone, a family-friendly area that includes Splash Island (a waterplay area), Waterside Theatre (an outdoor theatre) and Kids Zoo (a dynamic, interactive wildlife experience). The Toronto Zoo has over 16,000 animals (this includes insects and fish) and 491 species (not including invertebrates – animals without spinal columns) on 287 hectares (710 acres). It is one of the largest and best zoos in the whole world.

Cinesphere, the world's first IMAX cinema screen

In 1969, following a large plan to spruce up the Toronto waterfront, construction started on what would be called Ontario Place. It was the contribution of the Government of Ontario for this plan. Ontario Place was built on three artificial islands just off the shore, near the Canadian National Exhibition. Bridges over Lake Shore Boulevard connect the two parks. The purpose of the plan (reviving the waterfront and attracting tourists to the city) seems to have worked. Today the amusement park contains walkways, cafés, rides and theatres. Water attractions are a big part of Ontario Place, with a log ride, pedal boats, bumper boats, plenty of waterslides and more. It is a yearly favourite with Toronto families, so make sure you check it out! The newest addition to the park's program is the Chinese Lantern Festival, a highlight of late summer. Toronto's Festival started only in 2006, but is already a tradition. Hand-made by craftsmen from China, the silk lanterns are used to depict Chinese landmarks and mythology. The Festival also includes an authentic Chinese Marketplace, offering food from many regions of China.

Get this...

Cinesphere is the largest screen in the GTA with 800 seats • outer radius of 18.6 metres (61 feet) • walking paths were designed to ensure that comfortable rest areas were available for children and the elderly so that they would not need to walk too far without a seat • 100,000 lights are needed to illuminate the lanterns of the Chinese Lantern Festival! • over 14 kilometres (8.7 miles) of wire provide electricity to the lanterns • the schedule changes for optimal lighting

Marina Village

Fireworks

Chinese Lantern Festival

Humber Bay Park is a waterfront park located west of downtown Toronto. The park has two areas (called landspits) at the mouth of Mimico Creek. Humber Bay Park East is 19 hectares (47 acres) and Humber Bay Park West is 120 hectares (297 acres). Like Tommy Thompson Park, Humber Bay Park was created using lakefill. The Park contains cobble beaches, an outdoor structure for small performances, a waterfall, structured ponds, a state-of-the-art

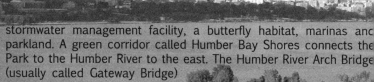

stormwater management facility, a butterfly habitat, marinas and parkland. A green corridor called Humber Bay Shores connects the Park to the Humber River to the east. The Humber River Arch Bridge (usually called Gateway Bridge) connects the Humber to Sir Casimir Gzowsky Park and Sunnyside Park, and the old city of Etobicoke to Toronto.

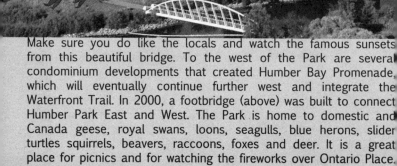

Make sure you do like the locals and watch the famous sunsets from this beautiful bridge. To the west of the Park are several condominium developments that created Humber Bay Promenade, which will eventually continue further west and integrate the Waterfront Trail. In 2000, a footbridge (above) was built to connect Humber Park East and West. The Park is home to domestic and Canada geese, royal swans, loons, seagulls, blue herons, slider turtles squirrels, beavers, raccoons, foxes and deer. It is a great place for picnics and for watching the fireworks over Ontario Place.

Aerial view of Humber Bay Park East,
Mimico Bridge and Toronto's skyline

Get this...

Mimico comes from the Native word "Omineca" which
means "home of the wild pigeons" ● the Park cost
$6.56 million ● when complete, the Waterfront Trail
will extend 900 kilometres from Niagara to Quebec

Get this...

the Market Gallery is locatd in what was once the City Council Chamber ● the first City Hall cost $52,000 ● the North St. Lawrence Market offers a farmers' market and an antique market ● St. Lawrence Hall contains businesses and City offices

The Flatiron in St. Lawrence is a Toronto icon

Toronto's first City Hall is now visible inside the larger market building

FRESH FISH

FISH SANDWICHES
SOLD HERE

The Town of York became the City of Toronto in 1834. A competition was held in 1844 for the construction of a City Hall. The new City Hall, which contained municipal offices, a farmers' market and Police Station #1, was completed in 1845. At that time, the building backed onto Lake Ontario. The city grew and by 1900, the population had reached more than 200,000 people. To accommodate the new population, City Hall was moved to a new City Hall (now known as Old City Hall) on Queen Street. In 1899, the St. Lawrence building was changed over 2 years into a large market. Because of its position on the south side of Front Street, the building became the South St. Lawrence Market. The building was renovated again in 1978. In 1979, The Market Gallery, the official exhibition facility for the City's art and archival collections, opened. For over a century St. Lawrence has been known for the variety of fresh fruits, vegetables, meat, fish, grains, baked goods, dairy products and great restaurants.

Yummy stuff

Furry farm cow

Young lamb

Riverdale Farm's history dates back to 1856, when it was to be Riverdale Park. In 1894 it became the Riverdale Zoo, Toronto's first zoo. It remained a zoo until 1974, when what is now known as Toronto Zoo opened in Scarborough (northeast of the city). The wild animals were moved to the new zoo at that time. In the following years, many of the buildings were removed, but it reopened in 1978 as Riverdale Farm. Today the farm provides Torontonians the chance to see how a farm really works. The Farm is in the heart of Cabbagetown (the old Irish neighbourhood) and is set on 3 hectares (7.5 acres), which include the farm, paths, ponds and gardens. Animals that live on the Farm include cows, horses, donkey, sheep, goats, pigs, chickens, turkeys, ducks, geese, rabbits and farm cats. Have you ever seen how a farmer milks a cow? Or what about a goat? Here's your chance! Watch the staff groom a horse. Eggs are collected from chickens every day. From May to October, the Friends of Riverdale Farm hold a farmers' market. Most food sold at the market is organic-certified and grown by the farmers themselves. Don't miss out on meeting some friendly creatures.

Get this!

the Zookeeper's House (now known as the "Residence")
was built in 1902 by prisoners of the Toronto Don Jail ●
the name Cabbagetown comes from the cabbages that
Irish immigrants grew in their front yards in the 1840s
● the farm is surrounded by an urban park with some
very murky ponds - watch the loons leaving a trail on
the yucky green surface as they swim around ● look
out for large mushroom colonies in the darker and
moister spots of the park, especially on the lower trunks
of trees - but pay attention, those mushrooms cannot be
eaten, and some may even be poisonous!!! ● all over
the world, horses are measured in hands, from the top
of the withers to the ground ● the maximum height for
a pony is 4 hands and 2 inches (over that, it's a horse!)

The BAPS Shri Swaminarayan Mandir is the first traditional stone Mandir in Canada. It was opened on July 22, 2007 by Prime Minister Stephen Harper, with other politicians present. BAPS Spiritual Leader Pramukh Swami Maharaj was also present. It took 2,000 builders, who were required to follow ancient Hindu rules for building holy shrines, 18 months to complete the building. A Mandir, the house of God, is a place of worship for all Hindus. There are only 8 BAPS Mandir outside India.

About Hinduism: Hinduism is one of the world's oldest religions and the third largest. Hindus call it "Sanatan Dharma". It is a belief and a way of life. The four beliefs of Sanatan Dharma are: Avatarvad (manifestation of God on earth), Murti Puja (worship of God's images and manifestations), Law of Karma (actions and their effects – good and bad) and Punarjanma (reincarnation). Hindus believe in one God (or Supreme Divinity). This God, however, incarnates on earth at different times – these incarnations are called avatars of God and each has a different name. These different names often confuse people into thinking Hindus believe in many Gods. But they do not.

Get this...

24,151 parts were hand-carved in India ● 10,000 tons of limestone, marble, sandstone and granite from India, Italy and Turkey were used ● the swastik cross (left) is an important Hindu symbol representing prosperity and well-being ● 5% of the population of Toronto are Hindus

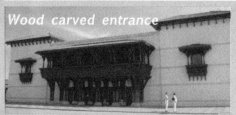

Wood carved entrance

Sculpted rooftops

The BAPS Mandir

Ontario pioneers

Winter in the village

Black Creek Pioneer Village began when the first European pioneers, Daniel and Elizabeth Stong, cleared the land and built a small log home in 1816. The family grew fast, as the Stongs had many children, and so did the farm. Several buildings were added, including a grain barn, a piggery, a smoke house and eventually a larger home to accommodate six sons and two daughters. Today, Black Creek Pioneer Village does not resemble the Stong family's original farm at all. Although the farm still stands, buildings have been added to form a more complete village. Most of the historic buildings were moved to the Village from surrounding communities around Toronto. These buildings have been restored and furnished to accurately represent that time. The Village allows you to experience how people lived in the 1860s. Look for people dressed in old clothes, and chat to them about life in the 19th century!

Get this...

Roblin's Mill is the only working water-powered mill in Toronto ● the Village has a collection of over 50,000 artifacts that represent late 18th and 19th century agricultural, economic, social and cultural developments of Upper Canada (now Ontario) ● back then, plants were used to create dyes – indigo was used to make blue, calendula to make orange, and blood root to make red ● dried tobacco was used in mattresses to get rid of bed bugs and between crops as a natural pesticide

The Lorraine Kimsa Theatre for Young People (once known as the Young People's Theatre) started over 40 years ago to produce high-quality professional productions written for children and their families. Classic or contemporary works from Canada and around the world are featured. The Theatre aims to inspire creativity, stimulate the imagination and instill the values of compassion, justice, beauty, truth, originality, hope and love. The Theatre puts on five to eight plays a season. Drama classes are also available. The building has an interesting past: it once housed the horses that pulled the city's streetcars. It was then turned into an electrical generation plant, and years later the Toronto Transit Commission (TTC) used the building as storage. In 1997, it became the home of LKTYP.

From the set of Pinocchio

Theatre for young people

Get this...

Toronto's oldest professional not-for-profit theatre ● *over 80,000 children attend shows at LKTYP every year* ● *the mainstage theatre seats 468* ● *darker coloured seats in the theatre are meant to fade away for the performers onstage* ● *costumes and sets are all made on-site*

Reference Section page 115

Toronto is often called Hollywood North. The City has studios for large and small productions, over 10,000 multicultural actors and diverse locations. This diversity, along with the City's ability to almost disappear on screen, has allowed Toronto to be used to represent many other cities. These include cities in the United States, Canada, Britain, France, Germany, Russia and Israel. On average, 18 productions are being filmed each day in Toronto. These include both Canadian and American productions. It's not uncommon to see streets lined with trailers, actors, directors and filming crews. Toronto is also home to the second most important film festival in the world (the Festival de Cannes is still on top!). The Toronto International Film Festival is held at the beginning of each September. Over 300 films from more than 50 countries are represented during the festival. The festival is open to the public as well as the industry. Hundreds of actors and directors come to the city where they can see the reaction of moviegoers to the premieres of their films.

Paparazzi

Film set

Get this...

over 340,000 people attend the festival each year • if you are in town, you may want to drop by the Roy Thompson Hall for some star-spotting! • walking around the city, you will often see small filming crews in the middle of streets • look out for the large white truck convoys (they mean big film production)

24

Entertainment District theatre

ROYAL
ALEXANDRA
THEATRE

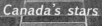
Canada's stars

CELINE DION

The initial idea of Canada's Walk of Fame was based on Hollywood's Walk of Fame (although there are now differences between the two). In 1998, the first group of inductees was inducted. Canada's Walk of Fame aims to honour accomplished Canadians. They include not only actors and musicians, but also models, painters, authors and athletes. The criteria for induction into Canada's Walk of Fame include: (1) must have been born in Canada or have spent their formative or creative years in Canada, (2) must have at least ten years experience in their field, (3) must have had national or international impact on Canada's Heritage. The Walk is located in the Entertainment District on King Street and Simcoe Street. Construction has begun on Celebration Park, the new home of Canada's Walk of Fame between Roy Thomson Hall (corner of King and Simcoe) and Metro Hall to the west.

Get this...

some actors thought to be American are actually Canadian ● individuals are inducted once a year during a group ceremony ● an individual can only have one star on the Walk - one exception is that an individual can also be inducted as part of a larger group ● nominations can be made by the public ● remember to look down and see if you can spot some names you know

名 唐 人 街

There are several Chinatowns in Toronto. The largest and oldest is located in the downtown area around Dundas Street West and Spadina Avenue. Toronto has the largest Chinese community in Canada and one of the largest in North America. The first Chinese settlers came to Canada in the 1870s to work on the Canadian Pacific Railway. When it was completed, many moved to Toronto where the community developed. This original Chinatown was located further east at Bay Street. However, construction of the new City Hall in the 1960s forced homes and businesses in the area to move west to its current location. The area is changing as younger Chinese move out and are replaced by Vietnamese, Thai and even Latin American immigrants. New Chinatowns have now appeared in Riverdale, Scarborough, Mississauga, North York, Richmond Hill and Markham and are growing.

The Lantern Festival celebrates
Chinese culture in Toronto

Get this...

there are over 500,000 Chinese in the GTA ● Chinese New Year is also called Spring Festival or Lunar New Year ● the Chinese Lantern Festival is a celebration held on the 15th day of the first month of the Lunar Year ● Chinese is not a single language, but rather a group of closely-related languages ● Mandarin and Cantonese are the most commonly-spoken languages in China as in Toronto ● Chinese is originally written from right to left in vertical columns ● fortune cookies originated in the U.S. and are not traditionally Chinese

With the largest Chinese community in Canada, Toronto is also home to the largest Chinese New Year festivities. The date changes every year, from late January to mid-February. Celebrations are held at the Canadian National Exhibition and include music, markets, food, drum and dragon performances and parades.

Spadina-Dundas Chinatown

East meets West

Get this...

over 9,072 kilograms (20,000 pounds) of Tiny Tim Donut dough are consumed yearly ● Cannonball Dave has blasted out of his cannon over 5,000 times ● butter sculptures in The Farm require 50 tonnes of butter ● the War of 1812 was fought on the site where the CNE now stands

CANADIAN NATIONAL
1879 EXHIBITION 1927

The Canadian National Exhibition (often called the "CNE" or "The Ex") was founded in 1879 as the Toronto Industrial Exhibition. Its purpose was to promote the development of agriculture, horticulture, arts, industry and commerce. In 1904, the name was unofficially changed to the Canadian National Exhibition. This change was made official in 1912. The Princes' Gates, the main entrance to the CNE, were

Midway

opened in 1927. Originally built to commemorate the 60th anniversary of Canadian Confederation, they were named in honour of Princes Edward and George. The gates include a central main arch, with nine pillars on each side, each representing a different Canadian province (Newfoundland was not a province at the time). CNE is now the largest annual fair in Canada. There are currently 60 rides on the Midway and 575 exhibitions to visit!

Candy kiosk

Fans of hockey can't miss the Hockey Hall of Fame. Watch clips of old games, Stanley Cup highlights, or the best moving hockey images in one of the theatres. Walk through the NHL Zone and learn about Honoured Members, new and old. For all you hockey players, why not try the NHLPA Be A Player Zone. Two interactive games allow you to go one-on-one against a life-sized computer simulation or become a goalie and defend your net from video images of hockey superstars. Any future hockey announcers out there? You can call the action at a hockey game in the Broadcast Zone. The MCI Great Hall showcases portraits and biographies of all honoured members as well as the NHL trophies, including The Stanley Cup. The original bowl of The Stanley Cup is now housed in Lord Stanley's Vault.

Stanley Cup

> ### Get this...
>
> *The Stanley Cup is over 100 years old and is the oldest trophy in North America ● it was donated in 1892*

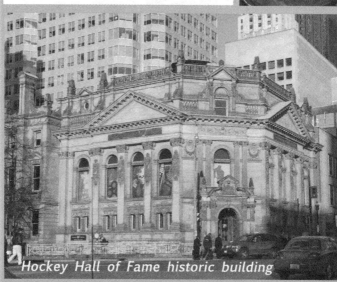

Hockey Hall of Fame historic building

According to the International Ice Hockey Federation, the first ice hockey match was played in Montréal's Victoria Rink on March 3, 1875. Written rules were first published in February 1877. More than 50 years later, hockey players and their achievements and contributions to the game began to be honoured (see Hockey Hall of Fame). While in Toronto, why not watch an exciting and chill-inducing live hockey game? The Toronto Maple Leafs are the city's hands-down favourites and play at the Air Canada Centre. But be prepared for an interesting time at the game – Torontonians are very passionate about their Maple Leafs! Games are often sold out, so plan ahead.

Goaltender

Get this...

the last Stanley Cup won by the Maple Leafs was in the 1966-67 season ● *the Leafs are sometimes called "the Buds"* ● *the Montréal Canadiens are the Leafs' greatest rivals*

The Rogers Centre is a stadium that is used for many things, primarily sports events, but also conventions, fairs and concerts. It has the world's first fully retractable roof, which allows it to be used during all seasons and in all weather conditions. It was opened in June 1989 as the SkyDome. It was renamed the Rogers Centre in 2005. There is a hotel and several restaurants in the Centre, including Windows, Sightlines, Arriba and the Hard Rock Café, all of which overlook the field. Want to eat something while you watch a game? The Rogers Centre is home to the Toronto Blue Jays baseball team and the Toronto Argonauts American football team. Grab a hot dog or a pretzel from one of the many food stands located in the Rogers Centre. Its unique architecture attracts questions from all over the world, including the U.S., the Netherlands, England, Germany, Australia, New Zealand, Singapore and China. Want to learn more about this one-of-a-kind facility? The Rogers Centre Tour Experience will take you behind the scenes and answer all your questions.

The roof

Get this...

a 31 storey building fits inside when the roof is closed! ● the roof opens or closes in 20 minutes ● it holds up to 55,000 people ● one of the world's largest videoboards, at 33.5 m (110 feet) wide by 10 m (33 feet) high

Baseball game

Skydome panoramic

The Air Canada Centre (usually called "The ACC") was built to house the Toronto Maple Leafs hockey team and the Toronto Raptors basketball team. It was built on the site of the Canada Post Delivery Building. It is now one of the top places for concerts in Toronto. The Raptors were established in 1995 when the NBA (National Basketball Association) expanded into Canada. They are the only Canadian team in the NBA. The name and colours for the team were chosen through the "Name Game", a Canada-wide contest. The top 10 list included: Beavers, Bobcats, Dragons, Grizzlies, Hogs, Raptors, Scorpions, T-Rex, Tarantulas and Terriers. The colours are bright red, purple, black and silver. Since 1995, basketball has increased in popularity and games are often nearly sold-out. Luckily tickets are usually available, so if you're a basketball fan, enjoy a game or two.

Get this...

the first hockey game at the ACC was played on February 20, 1999 ● first basketball game was played on February 21, 1999 ● first concert was on February 22, 1999 ● the ACC holds up to 19,800 people, depending on the event ● basketball was invented by Canadian James Naismith in 1891 ● the silver used in the uniforms is "Naismith silver"

Toronto Raptors' hom

Reference Section page 111

NBA game at the ACC

30

From December to March don't miss out on outdoor skating!

Skating is a popular winter activity in Toronto. Skating rink are located all over the city. The most famous is Natha Phillips Square's outdoor ice rink. The rink is open during the annual Cavalcade of Lights, a spectacular show happening a around you as you skate. The rink is open from November to March and rental skates are available. The Natrel Rink at the Harbourfront Centre is another popular ice rink. It is Canada' largest artificially cooled outdoor rink. Music plays as you skate Don't have your skates with you? The Centre can rent you pair. The rink opens in November. Kew Gardens in the Beac also has an outdoor skating rink. Why not go for a skate and then enjoy a hot chocolate in one of the Beach's cafés. Mak sure you bring your tuque and mitts! For all of you skiers ou there, you'll be happy to learn that there are two downhi skiing facilities in Toronto. Ski or snowboard your way dow the slopes at the North York Ski Centre or at Centennial Par Ski Area. Both offer ski and snowboard rental equipment. You' need your parents to do that for you. Lessons are also available

Get this...

many kids in Toronto (and Canada) learn how to skate when they are still toddlers ● *do not give up if you fall and smaller kids are wizzing around: everyone needs to learn!* ● *snow sports are very popular in Canada* ● *the country's Olympic teams usually bring home several medals* ● *contrary to what is commonly believed, Inuit languages do not have more words for snow than would be expected from a community living in the Great North*

Figure skating is a popular sport

Skiing in Centennial Park, yay!

Medieval Times Dinner & Tournament is a unique dining experience. While eating, watch a show like no other. Authentic costumes and weaponry adorn the Knights who compete on horseback. The night begins with an introduction to the 11th century by King Alfonso and his daughter, Princess Esperanza. You will receive a coloured crown that matches your seating area and the Knight that you will be cheering for during the show. Soon the Feast begins. Four courses are served by legions of wenches and serfs. There is no menu to chose from, but food includes garlic bread, vegetable soup, roasted chicken, spare ribs, a seasoned potato and dessert. In true medieval style, you won't see forks or knives during your meal! Back then, people ate with their hands, only using knifes to cut meat. The show begins while you eat. Six Knights compete in the tournament, which includes a flag toss, ring pierce and javelin throw. Next is the Joust. The Knights, in full armour and on horseback charge at each other with lances and broadswords, hoping to knock their opponents off their horses. Once off, the Knights battle it out using their swords, axes, maces and bolas (a spiked ball attached to a handle). When one Knight is left standing, he is declared the New Champion. But don't let yourself be fooled – the show is not over yet. About the show's swords: Two types are used during the show, the Espada and the Mandoble. The Espada is a one-handed short sword used while on horseback and often with a shield. The Mandoble is much heavier and requires two-hands.

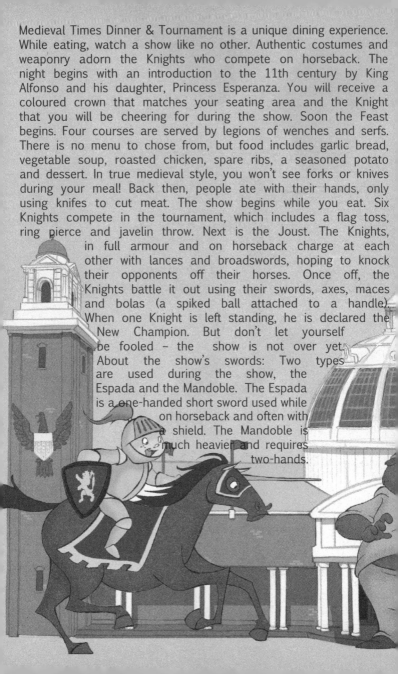

Get this...

the Medieval Times horses are Andalusians – purebred Spanish horses – used by royalty and knights since the 11th century ● Andalusian horses are said to be distant relatives of the highly intelligent Arabian horses ● the horses used in the show are raised and trained by Medieval Times ● over 375 hours of training are needed for performers to become Knights ● worn out weapons are replaced every 12 weeks

Codex Manesse

Jousting

A great way to experience Toronto's waterfront, especially in the summer, is by boat. Tour the harbour and enjoy the view of the City's skyline from the islands. To start your high seas adventure, take a walk along the Boardwalk at Queen's Quay and Harbourfront, where you'll find many boats willing to take you cruising. For something a little more personal and unique, why not try a private sailing yacht? Go for a private cruise, a family celebration, or learn sailing basics. You will need to work hard to persuade your parents though, as rentals are several hundred dollars. Alternatively, why not try a Hippo Tour? A Hippo is a unique amphibious vessel that can go on land and in water, giving you a safari-type tour. They are yellow, funny shapped and cute. Most tours stay in or around the harbour and the islands, but some will actually go all the way to Humber Bay. For those with more time, there are special, longer cruises in the Great Lakes

Kajama

Great Lakes schooner

Get this...

to see Toronto from Lake Ontario on the cheap, take the ferry to the Toronto Islands instead ● most boat tours depart from Harbourfront or Queen's Quay ● there are several old Great Lake Schooners available, as well as some Mississippi-style steamers ● if there are at least 6 of you, it may be worth calling a water taxi!

Toronto is often pointed out as the fourth best skyline in North America (after New York's, Chicago's and Los Angeles'). Touring the city by helicopter is a unique way to see it up close. There are dozens of new high rises being built, and you get to see all the movement. Helicopter tours usually depart from the City Centre Airport, just off Queen's Quay - you will need time to take a 2-minute ferry and clear security. During the CNE, helicopter tours also depart from the fair grounds. Longer tours can take you and your family all the way to Niagara Falls and back. Small airplane tours are also on offer!

Get this...

New York, Tokyo and Sao Paulo (Brazil) all have a reputation for having the largest helicopter fleets in the world ● media, leisure and rescue helicopters are often seen flying over Toronto, but usually not private ● on a jet helicopter, getting to Niagara Falls takes only 15-20 minutes, instead of more than one hour by car!

Toronto's urban sprawl

Central lake front

Business district

34

The Caribana festival is North America's biggest Caribbean Carnival-style event. Hundreds of thousands of tourists from all over the world come to participate and enjoy the festivities. Several weeks of celebrations end with a two-week "cultural explosion" and a final parade with boisterous dance in the streets. The parade is the highlight of the festival. Detailed colourful costumes are worn by dancers to make it a truly eye-catching Carnival experience. You'll hear many types of music, including soca (soul calypso), calypso, steelpan, reggae, and salsa. The bands are the most important part of the parade. They compete with each other on costume design, energy and creativity. It often takes a year to prepare the costumes, some of which are so large that those who wear them need someone to hold them from behind all the time!

Get this...

the parade attracts over 1 million people ● approximately 25,000 dancers participate each year ● started in 1967 ● modeled after Trinidad and Tobago's Carnival ● the whole West Indies community joins in

Caribana costumes

Get this...

almost 6,000 works of art make up the permanent
collection of the gallery ● 7,900 square metres (85,000
square feet) with 13 galleries, a theatre and a shop
● the property has 40 hectares (100 acres) ● the
gallery is committed to displaying only Canadian art
(both Group of Seven and Inuit and First Nations art)

Have you ever wondered about Canadian art? Visit the McMichael Canadian Art Collection to be introduced to Canada's art, history, people and cultures. The McMichael Collection was originally a private collection owned by Robert and Signe McMichael. Their private gallery grew and attracted many visitors. In 1965, realizing the importance of their collection, they donated it, along with their home and land, to the Province of Ontario. In 1966, the McMichael Conservation Collection of Art opened. The McMichael is the premier place to see works by Tom Thomson, the Group of Seven, their contemporaries (artists from the same period), and First Nations and Inuit artists. The McMichael is located in a woodland setting – the same setting that inspired much of the work on exhibit. To experience nature in a quiet setting, the McMichael offers several kilometres of trails for hikers, walkers and mountain bikers. The property is also home to the Tom Thomson Shack (the Toronto home of the artist which was later moved to the McMichael) and several outdoor sculptures, like the famous Inukshuk.

Island

Byng Inlet

Kwakwaka'wakw natives mask

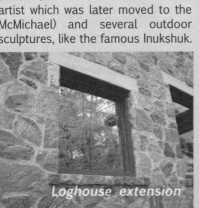
Loghouse extension

Inukshuk

Canada's Wonderland has over 200 attractions, 65 rides, Splash Works, live shows and more. The Park is made up of 10 themed areas: International Street, Grand World Exposition of 1890, Action Zone, Splash Works, White Water Canyon, KidZville, Hanna-Barbera Land, Nickelodeon Central, International Festival and Medieval Faire. The Park also contains the Kingswood Music Theatre with seating for 15,000 people. If you like water rides, be prepared to get soaked! Watch the Victoria Falls High Divers jump from the top of falls and perform amazing twists and turns in the air. Experience the thrill of Halloween like never before at the Park's Halloween Haunt.

Top Gun

Dragon-fire coaster

Get this...

Victoria Falls (on Wonder Mountain) powers the entire Park's air conditioning system ● over 100,000 foot-long hot dogs are consumed in a season ● North America's greatest variety of roller coasters, with 14 in all ● it would take 154,567,128 bottles of water to fill Splash Works ● the Behemoth, added for 2008, is Canada's biggest, fastest and tallest roller coaster, and North America's 6th largest

Did you ever wonder why stars twinkle at night? The reason is that the light bounces back and forth in our atmosphere and doesn't come straight to our eyes. This is just one of the interesting things you will learn when you visit the David Dunlap Observatory. The Observatory was a gift to the University of Toronto in 1935 with three objectives: astronomical research, training of advanced students at the University and encouraging public interest in astronomy. At the time, at 1.88 metres (74 inches) the telescope was the largest telescope in Canada and the second largest telescope in the world (the largest telescope was 2.54 metres (100 inches) and was located in California). The Administration building, which has two other reflector telescopes in the domes on top, contains facilities for analysing data as well as technical support. There are several types of telescopes: optical, radio, x-ray and gamma-ray. Optical telescopes are classified into three main types. They are: refracting, reflecting and catadioptric. Reflecting telescopes, like the ones used here, use mirrors to gather light and focus it to form an image.

Telescope dome

Get this...

the first black hole was observed and identified absorbing mass in 1971 from the Observatory – before this, black holes were just a theory ● the mirror in the telescope weighs 2,268 kilograms (5,000 pounds) ● lights in Richmond Hill were adopted to minimize light pollution

DAVID DUNLAP OBSERVATORY

Reference Section page 114

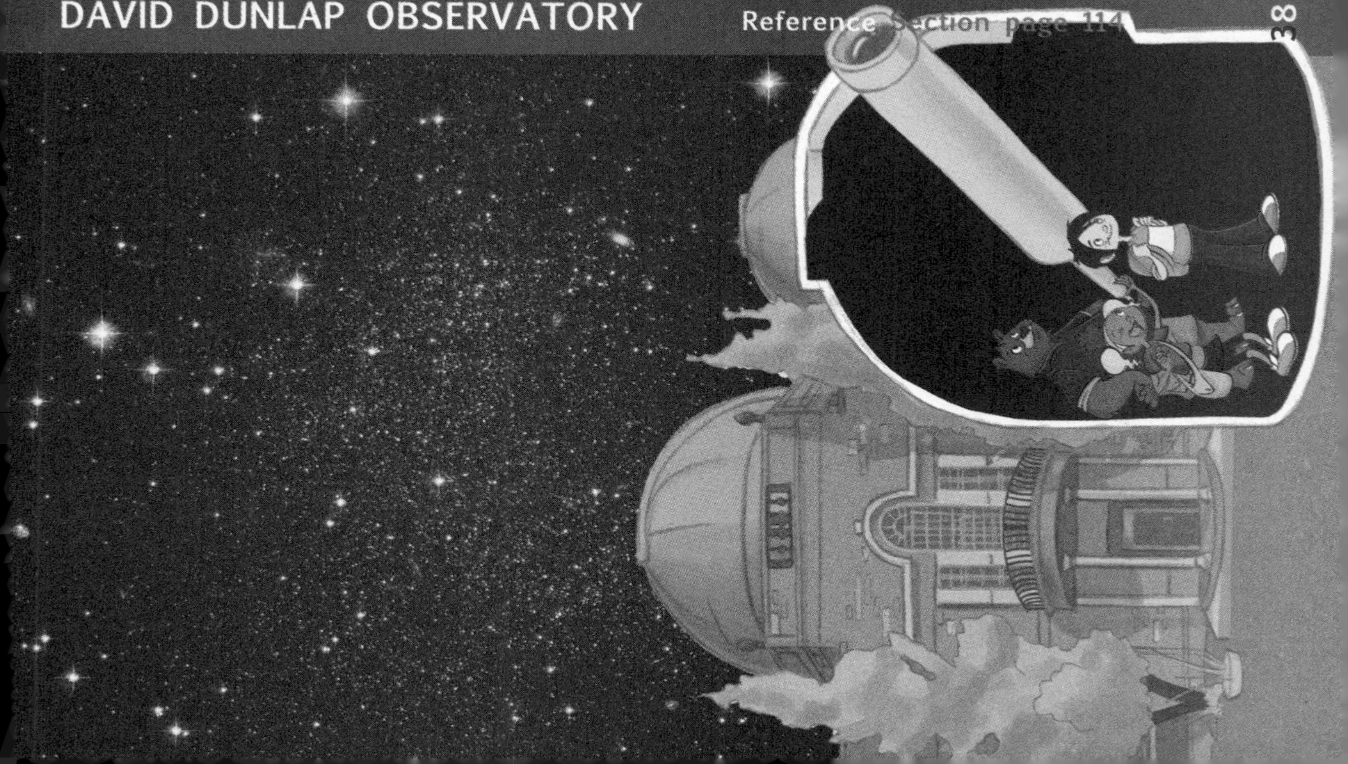

Get this...

the African word "safari" means to travel ● the cheetah is the fastest ground animal, reaching speeds up to 100 km/h (60 mph) in short sprints ● lions rest 90% of the day ● all the animals remain in the park during the winter ● a group of rhinos is called a "crash"

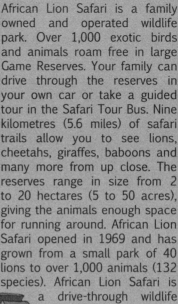

African Lion Safari is a family owned and operated wildlife park. Over 1,000 exotic birds and animals roam free in large Game Reserves. Your family can drive through the reserves in your own car or take a guided tour in the Safari Tour Bus. Nine kilometres (5.6 miles) of safari trails allow you to see lions, cheetahs, giraffes, baboons and many more from up close. The reserves range in size from 2 to 20 hectares (5 to 50 acres), giving the animals enough space for running around. African Lion Safari opened in 1969 and has grown from a small park of 40 lions to over 1,000 animals (132 species). African Lion Safari is a drive-through wildlife park dedicated to the conservation of declining wildlife species having successfully bred 20 species that are considered endangered and over 30 species that are threatened.

Lioness resting on a pride rock

The Welland Canal is a series of eight locks that connect Lake Ontario to Lake Erie. The Canal was built to allow ships to avoid Niagara Falls on their journey between the two lakes. The current Canal was built in 1932 and is the fourth series since 1829. The Welland Canals Centre, located at Lock 3, is the closest place to get to a ship travelling through the Great Lakes. Ships pass through daily. You don't want to miss the locks in action, so call ahead for a list of scheduled ships and times or just take your chance and try to see an unscheduled ship. Learn all about the system in the Centre. An area in the mueseum downstairs is also dedicated to lacrosse, a Canadian national sport.

Welland Canal museum

Lock 3

Get this!

the Canal is 43.5 kilometres (27 miles) long ● Lake Erie is 99.5 metres (326.5 feet) higher than Lake Ontario ● Lock 3 uses 93 million litres of water to raise and lower ships ● it takes 8-10 minutes to fill or empty Lock 3 ● Lock 3 is 261.8 metres (856 feet) long ● the Welland Canal is part of a larger navigation network called St. Lawrence Seaway System

St. Lawrence Seaway lock system

Lake Superior
185.5 m (602')

Lakes Huron & Michigan
176.3 m (578.5')

Lake Erie
174.5 m (572')

St. Marys River "Soo" Locks

St. Clair River Locks

64 m (210')

Welland Canal: 8 Locks

Lake Ontario
75.0 m (246')

Montréal/Lake Ontario Section: 7 Locks

St. Lawrence River
6.1 m (20')

SEA LEVEL

228.6 m (750')
382 m (925')

244.4 m (802')

406 m (1,332')

Old Port Dalhousie

There's lots to do in St. Catharines. Museums, historical sites, arts, culture, hiking trails, cycling, golfing, boating... the list goes on. And then there are the festivals, concerts and regattas. Drive or walk along the Heritage Corridor to learn St. Catharines' history. The Children's Discovery Centre of Niagara offers interactive exhibits and galleries such as Dinosaur and Hydro. If you're into walking or hiking, there's the St. Catharines Trail System. Over 90 kilometres (56 miles) of pathways crisscross through the city and the surrounding area. Port Dalhousie is the original site of the first three Welland Canals and now offers marinas, fishing charters, tour boats, beaches, picnic areas and more. www.stcatharines.ca

Montebello Park

Get this...

the city was the end of the Underground Railroad for hundreds of slaves from the U.S. in the 1820s ● often called The Garden City ● over 400 hectares (1,000 acres) of parks, gardens and trails ● was the home of the oldest winery in Canada ● the 100-year old Lakeside Park Carousel still costs a nickel (5 cents) to ride

Marineland is a park that offers a large selection of sea-creature entertainment. It is best known for its killer whales (orcas) and highly-trained dolphins. There are several areas and attractions in the park. Friendship Cove features Jump and Splash Sessions. Touch or feed a beluga whale in the Arctic Cove. The walruses and sea lions know how to put on a show for you. Animal displays include black bears, deer, buffaloes, elk and more! There are even rides like Dragon Mountain, the world's largest steel roller coaster and Sky Screamer, the world's highest triple tower ride.

Get this...

despite their name, killer whales are actually friendly and affectionate ● *unlike most other whales, the belugas' seven neck vertebrae are not fused, allowing them to nod and turn their heads* ● *walruses can dive to depths of 90 metres (300 feet) and stay under for up to half an hour* ● *sea lions were worshipped by ancient Peruvians*

Underwater meeting with the orcas

Canadian Falls or "Horseshoe Falls"

New York State, United States of America

Niagara Falls is Canada's top tourist attraction, and a visit to Toronto would not be complete without a day at the Falls. The Niagara River forms the border between Canada and the U.S. The river connects Lake Ontario to Lake Erie. Niagara Falls is made up of the American Falls and the Canadian, or Horseshoe, Falls. Both falls face Canada, giving visitors in Ontario the best views. Because of the power and speed of the water near the Falls, hydroelectric plants have been built along the river on both sides to generate power. The U.S. is directly across the river and is accessible via the Rainbow Bridge, which connects Niagara Falls, Ontario to Niagara Falls, New York. Don't forget your passport!

Get this...

*the Falls attract over 12 million visitors a year ●
the water is gradually eroding the Falls ● Horseshoe
Falls are 52 metres (170 feet) high ● crestline is
670 metres (2,200 feet) ● depth of the river at the
Falls is also 52 metres (170 feet) ● during high
flow, more than 168,000 cubic metres (6 million
cubic feet) of water go over the Falls every minute*

Winter view

The edge of the falls

Horseshoe Falls from the air

There are plenty of things to do at Niagara Falls. The Maid of the Mist takes you on a half-hour adventure through the mist and up close to the base of the Horseshoe Falls. Put on the recyclable rain poncho and be ready to get wet! Want to see more? Journey Behind the Falls takes you 46 metres (150 feet) deep into the solid rock to tunnels that take you behind the Falls. Put on your poncho again and watch the water as it rushes past at 65 kilometres per hour just a few feet away from where you stand. Listen to the sound of water hitting the river from the observation deck at the foot of the Falls. The Falls have inspired many daredevils to perform crazy and unbelievable stunts. People have jumped, gone over the Falls in a barrel, crossed the Falls on a tightrope. Some have gone over the Falls unintentionally. Learn more at the IMAX Theatre Niagara Falls & Daredevil Gallery. The latest stunt was an unsuccessful attempt to drive a golf ball over Niagara Falls (approximately 362 yards).

Get this...

each Maid of the Mist boat holds 600 passengers ●
first Maid of the Mist made its journey in 1846 ● it
is one of North America's oldest tourist attractions ●
one-fifth of the world's fresh water flows over Niagara
Falls ● it is illegal in both Canada and the U.S. to go
over the Falls ● in 2003, the last person to go over
the Falls did so with no safety device and survived

OF THE MIST

American Falls in the winter time

The White Water Walk lets you walk along class 6 white-water rapids, the fastest and most violent on earth. Here the water travels at about 48 kilometres per hour (30 miles per hour). But be careful and don't get too close! The antique Whirlpool Aero Car takes you high above the whirling water in the river below. During the 10 minute trip, you will briefly enter the U.S. But don't worry – you won't need your passport! The Skylon Tower is the tallest structure in Niagara. Enjoy the views from 236 metres (775 feet) above the Falls. A glass elevator takes you to the top. And if that's not enough for you, there are helicopter tours that take you high above the Horseshoe. You'll definitely want to have your camera with you for this! As a top tourist destination, the Falls are now surrounded by hotels, entertainment, restaurants, amusement areas, rides and more. This area, known as Clifton Hill, also offers attractions such as the Canadian Midway, Movieland Wax Museum, Ghost Blasters and Dinosaur Park. Stay an extra day to experience it all! For the nature lover in you, there's the Niagara Garden Trail with a butterfly conservatory, floral showhouse, botanical gardens and flower clock.

White Water Walk experience

Skylon

Sneaky way to USA

Lots of tall hotels and casinos

Raging rapids in US side

Reference Section pages 116-118

The following pricing and contact information is accurate at the time of publishing It should be considered as guideline information only. Junior Jetsetters advises the consultation of the respective websites for up-to-date information, as prices may change without warning. There may also be tax(es) on top of the listed price. Payment methods that may be accepted include American Express (AmEx), MasterCard (MC), Visa (V), Diners Club (DC), debit/bank cards (Interac) and travellers' cheques (TC). Many shops, attractions and restaurants accept US currency. All prices are in Canadian dollars.

CITY PASS

Tel (707) 256-0490
www.citypass.com
Price Adults $59, Youth (4-12) $37. **Credit** AmEx, MC, V, Interac.

AFRICAN LION SAFARI

1386 Cooper Rd., Flamborough,
Tel (519) 623-2620
Fax (519) 623-9542
www.lionsafari.com
Open May-June 10am-4pm Mon-Fri, 10am-5pm Sat-Sun, June-Labour Day 10am-5:30pm daily, Sept-Oct 10am-4pm daily. Ticketbooth opens 9am daily. **Closed** Oct-May **Admission** summer: Adults $26.95, Children (3-12) $21.95, spring/fall: Adults $21.95, Children (3-12) $16.95. **Credit** MC, V, Interac.

AIR CANADA CENTRE

40 Bay Street
Tel (416) 815-5500
Fax (416) 359-9332
www.theaircanadacentre.com
Tickets Toronto Maple Leafs (hockey), Toronto Raptors (basketball) & Toronto Rock (lacrosse): (416) 872-5000
www.mapleleafs.com
www.raptors.com
www.torontorock.com
For information on music and variety shows, consult the ACC website above.

ART GALLERY OF ONTARIO or AGO

317 Dundas Street West
Tel (416) 979-6648

www.ago.net
Open 10am-9pm Wed-Fri, 10am-5:30pm Sat-Sun. **Closed** Mon-Tues. **Admission** Adults \$15, Youths (6-15) \$10. **Credit** MC, V, Interac.

BAPS SHRI SWAMINARAYAN MANDIR

61 Claireville Drive
Tel (416) 798-2227
Fax (416) 798-4498
www.baps.org & kids.baps.org
Open 9am-6pm daily.
Admission free.
The Mandir is a working religious temple, where strict rules of conduct shoud be observed, notably in what concerns dress code, shoes, photography/video, cell phones, food/drink and smoking. For more information refer to the full rules before visiting: www.swaminarayan.org/globalnetwork/america/toronto.htm

BLACK CREEK PIONEER VILLAGE

1000 Murray Ross Parkway
Tel (416) 736-1733
Fax (416) 661-6610
www.blackcreek.ca
Open May-June 9:30am-4pm Mon-Fri, 11am-5pm Sat-Sun, July-Labour day (1st Monday in September) 10am-5pm Mon-Fri, 11am-5pm Sat-Sun, Labour Day-Dec 31 9:30am-4pm Mon-Fri, 11am-4:30pm Sat-Sun. **Closed** December 25 and 26 **Admission** Adults \$13, Children (15 and under) \$9. **Parking** \$6 (cash). **Credit** AmEx, MC, V, Interac.

CANADA'S WALK OF FAME

King Street West & Simcoe Street (look for the stars on the sidewalks surrounding Roy Thompson Hall, Royal Alexandra Theatre and Princess of Wales Theatre)
Tel (416) 367-9255
Fax (416) 367-0090
www.canadaswalkoffame.com

CANADA'S WONDERLAND

9580 Jane Street, Vaughan
Tel (905) 832-8131
www.canadaswonderland.com
Open May-Oct daily. **Closed** Nov-Apr. **Admission** Adults and over 48" tall \$51.40, Children under 48" tall \$24.95, **Parking** \$10. **Credit** AmEx, MC, V, Interac.

CANADIAN NATIONAL EXHIBITION (CNE), THE EX

Lake Shore Boulevard West & Strachan Avenue
Tel (416) 393-6300
www.theex.com
Open last 18 days of summer, ending Labour Day (1st Monday of September), Gates open 10am-10pm, Grounds 10am-12midnight. **Closed** Sept-mid Aug. **Admission**

Adults $14, Children (2-13) $10, rides, food and beverages extra, Ride pass: $31 (plus admission). Advance tickets available online.

CARIBANA

Various locations
Tel (416) 391-5608
www.caribanafestival.com
Festival takes place over several weeks in July-Aug. The main parade occurs on a Sunday in August. Check website in advance for dates, locations and ticket information for the street parades and special events.

CASA LOMA

1 Austin Terrace
Tel (416) 923-1171
Fax (416) 923-5734
www.casaloma.org
Open 9:30am-5:00pm daily (last admission 4:00pm), Gardens May to October. **Closed** December 25. **Admission** Adults $16, Children (4-13) $8.75, Youth (14-17) $10. **Parking** $2.75/hour, $8.25 max. **Credit** AmEx, MC, V, DC.

CENTREVILLE

Centre Island
Tel (416) 203-0405
Fax (416) 203-2167
www.centreisland.ca
Ferry from Queen's Quay.

Open (weather permitting) June-Labour Day (1st Monday in Sept) 10:30am, closing times vary, May & Sept 10:30-6pm Sat-Sun only. **Closed** Oct-Apr. **Admission** free to park (excludes rides), Ride passes: Adults $27.50, Children (under 4 feet) $19. **Credit** MC, V, Interac.

CHINESE LANTERN FESTIVAL

Ontario Place, 955 Lakeshore Boulevard West
Tel (416) 314-9900
Fax (416) 314-9989
www.chineselanternfestival.ca
Open mid-July-Oct, call for schedule. **Closed** Oct-mid-July. **Admission** Adults $25, Children (4-12) $20. **Credit** AmEx, MC, V, Interac.

CN TOWER

301 Front Street West
Tel (416) 868-6937
Fax (416) 601-4722
www.cntower.ca
Open 10am-10pm daily. **Admission** Total Tower Experience (Look Out, Glass Floor, Skypod, Movie, Motion Theatre Ride) $31.99, Observation Sky Pod Experience (Look Out, Glass Floor, Skypod) Adults $25.99, Children (4-12) $19.99. **Credit** AmEx, MC, V, Interac.
Look out for tower light shows on certain civic holidays (free).

DAVID DUNLAP OBSERVATORY

Hillsview Drive, Richmond Hill
Tel (905) 884-9562 ext. 232
Fax (905) 884-2672
www.astro.utoronto.ca/DDO/
Open May-Oct, Fri-Sat
evenings only. Call ahead to
confirm times and reserve.
Closed Nov-Apr & May-Oct,
Sun-Thurs. **Admission** Adults
$6, Children (7-12) $4. Children
under 7 not permitted,
as the DDO is a working
research facility. Cash only.
Price includes astronomy
lecture and visit to the main
telescope dome. Weather
allowing, guests are invited to
look through the telescope.
Tip: alternatively, ask for (free)
visits to one of the small
telescope domes upstairs in
the main building.

FORT YORK

100 Garrison Road
Tel (416) 392-6907
Fax (416) 392-6917
Event Hotline (416)338-3888
www.toronto.ca/culture/
fort_york.htm
Open Labour Day (1st Monday
in September)-Victoria Day
(end of May) 10am-4pm
Mon-Fri, 10am-5pm Sat-Sun,
Victoria Day-Labour Day
10am-5pm daily. **Closed**
last two weeks in December.
Check website for other
closing dates and special
events. Daily calendar posted
at the entrance, different
tours and demonstrations
available several times daily.
Admission Adults $6, Children
(under 12) $3, Youths (13-18)
$3.25. **Parking** free. **Credit**
AmEx, MC, V, Interac.

HARBOURFRONT CENTRE

235 Queens Quay West
Tel (416) 973-4000
www.harbourfrontcentre.com
Open 9am-6pm daily, see
Info Desk for details. Activities
and performances, arts &
crafts courses, outdoor
markets, concerts, canoeing,
ice-skating, exhibitions in the
old power plant building. Ask
for a program.

HOCKEY HALL OF FAME

Brookfield Place (formerly
BCE Place), 30 Yonge Street
Tel (416) 360-7765
www.hhof.com
Enter on -1, inside shopping
area. **Open** 10am-5pm Mon-
Fri, 9:30-6pm Sat, 10:30am-
5pm Sun. **Closed** December
25, January 1, Induction
Day (1 day each November)
& December 25. Look out
for special Induction Day
events, and come by to see
the newest hockey stars up
close, when they are added
to the wall and sign the
book. **Admission** Adults $13,
Youths (4-13) $9. **Credit**

AmEx, MC, V, Interac.

LEGISLATIVE ASSEMBLY OF ONTARIO

Legislative Building
Queen's Park
Tel (416) 325-7500
Fax (416) 325-7489
www.ontla.on.ca
Open 8:30am-5pm Mon-Fri (year round), 9am-4:30pm Sat-Sun Victoria Day weekend-Labour Day weekend. Call ahead in the day of your visit for tour times. Different tours available. **Admission** free. When in session, visitors are welcome to watch the public debates from the guest galleries. The House meets Monday through Thursday from 1:30pm to 6pm and on Thursday mornings from 10am to 12noon.

LORRAINE KIMSA THEATRE FOR YOUNG PEOPLE

165 Front Street East
Tel (416) 363-5131
Fax (416) 363-5136
Box office (416) 862-2222
www.lktyp.ca

Open Oct-May (plays), June-Sept (drama school), box office 9am-5pm Mon-Fri & 9am-5pm Sat-Sun on performance days only. **Closed** non-performance weekend days. **Admission** Adults $20, Children (1-18)

$15 (additional handling fee may apply). **Credit** AmEx, MC, V, Interac.

MARINELAND

7657 Portage Road, Niagara Falls (1 mile away from Horseshoe Falls)
Tel 905-356-9565
www.marinelandcanada.com
Open Ticket booth open summer 9am-6pm, mid-season 10am-5pm, park attractions remain open until nightfall. **Closed** winter (check website for specific dates). **Admission** Adults $38.95, Youths (5-9) $31.95, Children under 4 free. If you are in the Niagara region for a while, ask for the Marineland Fun Card Season's Pass - an extra $5 will buy get you as many times as you want through the season. **Parking** free. **Credit** AmEx, MC, V, Interac.

McMICHAEL COLLECTION OF CANADIAN ART

10365 Islington Avenue, Kleinburg
Tel (905) 893-1121
Fax (905) 893-2588
www.mcmichael.com
Open 10am-4pm Mon-Sat, 10am-5pm Sun. **Closed** December 25. **Admission** Adults $15, Students $12. **Parking** $5 (cash only). **Credit** AmEx, MC, V, Interac.

MEDIEVAL TIMES DINNER & TOURNAMENT

Exhibition Place
Tel (888) 935-6878
or (888) WE-JOUST
www.medievaltimes.com
Open schedule varies – call for reservations **Admission** Adults $59.95, Children (12 and under) $39.95.

NATHAN PHILLIPS SQUARE

100 Queen Street West
Tel (416) 338-0338
Fax (416) 338-0685
www.toronto.ca/city_hall_tour/index.htm
Toronto City Hall: **Open** 8:30am-4:30pm Mon-Fri **Closed** Sat-Sun **Admission** free. Nathan Phillips Sq.: **Open** daily.

NIAGARA FALLS

The following list includes only a small number of Niagara's attractions. Junior Jetsetters advises you to drop by the Niagara Falls Visitor Centre when you first arrive, to learn about all the possibilities on the Canadian side. Ask about the Passport to the Falls (good deal for several attractions). Or try the Niagara Falls & Great Gorge Adventure Pass (Maid of the Mist, White Water Walk, Butterfly Conservatory, People Mover Bus, and discounts to other attractions): Adults $43.13, Youth (6-12) $26.94. More information is available at www.niagaraparks.com and www.infoniagara.com.

Cirque Niagara's Avaia

Toll Free (877) 247-7831
www.cirqueniagara.com
Admission Adults $39-$79, Youth (under 12) $19.50-$39.50, one kid free per couple, 50% off any extra children.

Heli Tours

Toll Free (800) 491-3117
www.nationalhelicopters.com/niagara
Admission Adults $139, Youth (under 12) $85, Family Pass $360 for 2 adults and 2 youth under 12, extra kids $70, kids under 3 free. Price is for a 20 minute tour over the falls. Bring your camera!

Journey Behind the Falls

www.niagaraparks.com
Open Year round, except Dec 25. **Admission** Adults $12, Youth (6-12) $7.20. Prices may be lower if icing conditions cause the lower observation deck to close.

Konica Minolta Tower Centre

Toll Free (800) 461-2492
www.niagaratower.com
Open every day until late in the night. **Admission**

Single/Return (2 trips) Adult 6.95/$8.95, Youth (6-18) 4.95/$6.95. Observation deck and restaurant overlooking the Horseshoe Falls at 160.02 m.

Maid of the Mist

Tel (905) 358-5781
www.maidofthemist.com
Open Apr-Oct (depends on ice conditions in the river) **Admission** Adult $14, Youth (6-12) $8.60.

Oh Canada Eh? Dinner Show

Toll Free (800) 467-2071
www.ohcanadaeh.com
Admission (dinner and show, does not include tips) Adult $49.95, Youth $26.10. An unforgettable musical celebration of Canada, featuring singing Mounties, lumberjacks, hockey players, Anne of Green Gables and others.

Ripley's Niagara

4960 Clifton Hill
www.ripleysniagara.com
Check website for information on Ripley's Believe it or Not!, Louis Tussaud's and Ripley's Moving Theatre.

Sir Adam Beck 2 Generator Station

www.niagaraparks.com
Open for summer season only

Admission Adults $8.50, Youth (6-12) $5.

Skylon Tower

Tel (905) 356-2651
www.skylon.com
Open summer 8am-12midnight, winter 9am-10pm **Admission** Adult $10.95, Youth $6.45. Watch the falls from high up in the sky pod.

Whirlpool Aero Car

3850 Niagara River parkway
www.niagaraparks.com
Open Mar-Nov, depending on weather conditions. **Admission** Adult $11, Youth (6-12) $6.50. Enter the U.S. briefly.

White Water Walk

www.niagaraparks.com
Open Mar-Oct 9am until dusk. **Admission** Adult $8.50, Youth (6-12) $5. One of the world's only Level 6 rapids.

Whirlpool Jet

Toll Free (888) 438-4444
www.whirlpooljet.com
Admission Adult $56, Youth (6-13) $47 (minimum height restrictions). Experience the Niagara River at high speed. You will get (very) wet!

Zooz Animal Park

Stevensville
(10 minutes from the Falls)
Toll Free (866) 367-9669
www.zooz.ca
Open May-Oct. **Closed** winter season. **Admission** Adult $17.50, Youth (4-12) $13.

ONTARIO PLACE

955 Lakeshore Boulevard W
Tel (416) 314-9900
Fax (416) 314-9989
www.ontarioplace.com
Open May 10am-6pm Sat-Sun only, June 10am-5pm (7pm Sat-Sun), July-Aug 10am-7pm daily, Sept 10am-6pm Sat-Sun only **Closed** May & Sept Mon-Fri, Oct-Apr. **Admission** Adults $12.75, Children 6-13) $12.75, Children (4-5) $6.75, Ride pass Ages 4 and up $45, **Parking** $12-20. **Credit** AmEx, MC, V, Interac.

ONTARIO SCIENCE CENTRE

770 Don Mills Road
Tel (416) 696-1000
www.ontariosciencecentre.ca
Open 10am-5pm daily. **Closed** December 25. **Admission** Adults $17, Children (4-12) $10, Youth (13-17) $12.50, **Parking** $8 (cash only). **Credit** AmEx, MC, V, Interac.

RIVERDALE FARM

201 Winchester Street
Tel (416) 392-6794
Fax (416) 392-0329,
www.toronto.ca/parks/
riverdalefarm.htm
Open 9am-5pm daily **Admission** free. Once you are there, visit the adjacent swamp and trails, and look for some serious wildlife

ROGERS CENTRE (SKYDOME)

1 Blue Jays Way
Tel (416) 341-1707
Fax (416) 341-3110
www.rogerscentre.com
Tours: **Open** year round (call for schedule – (416) 341 2770). **Closed** depending on event schedule. **Admission** Adults $13.50, Children (5-11) $8, Youth (12-17) $9.50 **Credit** AmEx, MC, V, Interac **Tickets** Toronto Blue Jays (baseball) (416) 341-1234 Toronto Argonauts (American football) (416) 341-2746 toronto.bluejays.mlb.com
www.argonauts.ca

ROYAL ONTARIO MUSEUM (ROM)

100 Queen's Park
Tel (416) 586-8000
www.rom.on.ca
Open 10am-5:30pm Sat-Thurs, 10am-9:30pm Fri 10am-4pm December 24 &

1. **Closed** December 25 & January 1. **Admission** Adults 20, Children (5-14) $14, Audio Tour $5 (plus admission). **Credit** AmEx, MC, V, Interac.

SKATING & SKIING

Skating:
Nathan Phillips Square
100 Queen Street West
Tel (416) 392-1111
Kew Gardens, Lee Avenue
Tel (416) 392-0740
For other locations:
Tel (416) 338-7465
www.toronto.ca/parks/recreation_facilities/skating/skating.htm
Open Nov-Mar daily. **Closed** Mar-Nov. **Admission** free.

Skiing:
North York Ski Centre
Earl Bales Park
4169 Bathurst Street
Tel (416) 395-7934
www.toronto.ca/parks/recreation_facilities/skiing/northyorkski.htm
Open Dec-Mar (weather permitting) 1pm-9:30pm Mon, 10am-9:30pm Tues-Fri, 9am-8pm Sat, 9am-6pm Sun. **Closed** Apr-Nov, December 25. **Admission** Adults $14 for 1 hour, Juniors (5-14) $11 for 1 hour, Students (15-18) $12 for 1 hour, Equipment rental extra. **Credit** MC, V, Interac.

Centennial Park Snow Centre
Centennial Park

256 Centennial Park Road
Tel (416) 394-8750
www.toronto.ca/parks/recreation_facilities/skiing/centennialski.htm
Open Dec-Mar (weather permitting) 10am-9:30pm Mon-Fri, 9am-9pm Sat, 9am-6pm Sun. **Closed** Apr-Nov. **Admission** $10 for 1 hour, Equipment rental extra. **Credit** MC, V, Interac.

ST. LAWRENCE MARKET

South Market
95 Front Street East
Tel (416) 392-7120
Fax (416) 392-0120
www.stlawrencemarket.com
Open 8am-6pm Tues-Thurs, 8am-7pm Fri, 5am-5pm Sat. **Closed** Sun-Mon.

Market Gallery, 2nd Floor,
95 Front Street East
Tel (416) 392-7604
Fax (416) 392-0572
stlawrencemarket.com/gallery
Open 10am-4pm Wed-Fri, 9am-4pm Sat, 12noon-4pm Sun. **Closed** Mon-Tues. **Admission** free.

TOMMY THOMPSON PARK

Leslie Street (south of Lake Shore Boulevard East)
Tel (416) 661-6600
www.trca.on.ca
Open weekends & holidays only, Apr-Oct 9am-6pm, Nov-Mar 9am-4:30pm.

Closed weekdays year-round, December 25, 26 & January 1. **Admission** free.

TORONTO ISLANDS

www.toronto.ca/parks/island/ & www.torontoisland.org
Open year-round. Admission free. Ferry (round trip) Adults $6, Juniors (under 14) $2.50, Students (under 19) $3.50. The docks are located at the foot of Bay Street at Queens Quay, just west of the Westin Harbour Castle Hotel. Check the schedule at www.toronto.ca/parks/island/

TORONTO ZOO

361A Old Finch Avenue
Tel (416) 392-9101
Fax (416) 392-5863
www.torontozoo.com
Open Oct-Mar 9:30am-4:30pm daily, Mar-Oct 9am-6pm (7:30pm Victoria Day-Labour Day) daily. **Closed** December 25. **Admission** Adults $20, Children (4-12) $12, **Parking** $8. **Credit** AmEx, MC, V, Interac.

WELLAND CANAL

Lock 3, 1932 Welland Canals Parkway, St. Catharines
Tel (905) 984-8880
stcatharineslock3museum.ca
Open 9am-5pm daily.
Admission Adults $4.25, Children (6-13) $2.50.

TORONTO BY HELICOPTER

The Helicopter Company
Toronto City Centre Airport
Tel (416) 203-3280
Fax (416) 203-3282
www.helitours.ca
Open all year. **Price** $90 for 7 minutes, $170 for 16 minutes (per person). **Credit** MC, V

TORONTO BY BUS

Gray Line
300-180 Dundas Street West
Tel (416) 594-3310
www.grayline.ca
Open 9am-4pm daily. **Price** Adults $34, Children (5-11) $18. **Credit** AmEx, MC, V
Note: Tours start at 123 Front Street West & 610 Bay Street

TORONTO BY BOAT

Mariposa Cruises
415-207 Queen's Quay West
Tel (416) 203-0178

www.mariposacruises.com
Open Harbour Tours: May-Sept starting at 11am daily. **Price** Adult $18.87, Children (4-11) $13.21, Students (12-17) $16.98. **Credit** AmEx, MC, V. (Other tours available).

Great Lakes Schooner Co.
111-249 Queen's Quay West
Tel (416) 260-6355
Fax (416) 260-6377
www.greatlakesschooner.com
Open June 3pm Mon-Fri, 11:30am, 1:30pm, 3:30pm Sat & Sun, July-Sept 11:30am, 1:30pm, 3:30pm daily. **Price** Adult $19.95, Children $10.95. **Credit** Amex, MC, V, DC.

Sailing For You
Pier 2, Queen's Quay West
Tel (416) 276-9343
www.sailingforyou.ca
Open call for availability. Price 4 hours and up to 6 passengers starting at $695, 7-8 passengers starting at $795, 9-10 passengers starting at $925.

Hippo Tours
151 Front Street West
Tel (416) 703-4476
Fax (416) 868-4476
www.torontohippotours.com
Open May-Oct 11am-5pm daily. **Price** Adults $38, Children (3-12) $25, Students (13-17) $33. **Credit** AmEx, MC, V. See Toronto from Lake Ontario and from the road, without ever leaving your Hippo!

Luxury

FAIRMONT ROYAL YORK HOTEL

100 Front Street West
Toll Free (800) 257-7544
Tel (416) 368-2511
Fax (416) 368-9040
www.royalyorkhotel.com
Credit AmEx, DC, MC, V, Interac. An opportunity to stay right at the heart of Toronto, and if you are lucky, walk amid presidents, kings, queens, princes and movie stars. If you are royalty yourself, splurge in the ultra-expensive Royal Suite!

RENAISSANCE TORONTO HOTEL DOWNTOWN AT THE ROGERS CENTRE/SKYDOME

1 Blue Jays Way
Toll Free (800) 237-1512
Tel (416) 341-7100
Fax (416) 341-5091

See attraction pages for more information

www.marriott.com

Credit AmEx, DC, MC, V, Interac. If you are a sports fan, then this hotel is for you. Right in the city centre, it is built into the Rogers Centre, with some of the rooms looking onto the pitch. Check game schedules and watch the Blue Jays from your own window (rest assured, cameras have no angle to look in though!). Ask for the Toronto Blue Jays package and the CN Tower Lookout Package.

Expensive

DELTA CHELSEA

33 Gerrard Street West
Toll Free (877) 814-7706
Tel (416) 595-1975
Fax (416) 585-4375
www.deltachelsea.com

Credit AmEx, DC, MC, V, Interac. At the corner of Bay and Gerrard, this is one of the largest hotels in the British Commonwealth. Anything you can think of is available. The hotel is extremely kid-friendly, and includes child-care with petting bunnies, video arcade, swimming pool with its own water slide and a wading pool. Kids under 17 can stay for free with their parents. Try one of the family rooms (bunk-beds and other family layouts).

THE SUTTON PLACE HOTEL

955 Bay Street
Toll Free (800) 268-3790
Tel (416) 924-9221
Fax (416) 924-1778
www.suttonplace.com

Credit AmEx, DC, MC, V, Interac. One of Toronto's classics, the Sutton goes for an old-world style luxury. If you are coming during the Toronto International Film Festival, this is the place to stay for some star-spotting. Mind you, in Hollywood North, the Sutton hosts stars all year round. Try your luck.

THE WESTIN HARBOUR CASTLE

1 Harbour Square
Toll Free (888) 325-5144
Tel (416) 869-1600
Fax (416) 869 0573
www.starwood.com/westin/index.html

Credit AmEx, DC, MC, V, Interac. The Westin is not one the glitziest in Toronto, but has above-average service for families with children. As the building is located right on the lake, make sure you get a room facing south, for views of The Island! Several restaurants on premises, but try out the Toulà Restaurant and Bar atop the South Tower, in a rotating pod. You should be able to see The Island and

Toronto's business centre throughout dinner.

Moderate

BEACHES BED & BREAKFAST

174 Waverley Road
Tel (416) 699-0818
Fax (416) 699-2246
members.tripod.com/beachesbb/
Credit AmEx, MC, V, Interac. Right off Queen Street East, this B&B is perfect for life at the Toronto Beach, literally just steps away. The neighbourhood is slow-paced and full of character. Access the city centre by taking streetcar 501 to Lake Shore. Only for cat-lovers: Enid, the owner, has three cats in the property.

THE CASA LOMA INN

21 Walmer Road
Tel (416) 924-4540
Fax (416) 975-5485
Credit cards not accepted. Make sure your cab driver got the address right, or you may be dropped off at the Other Casa Loma - the castle! This is a full of character 1885 Victorian house, conveniently located at St. Clair Avenue. Rooms have microwaves and fridges.

Budget

AINSLEY HOUSE BED & BREAKFAST

19 Elm Avenue
Tel (888) 423-3337 / (416) 972-0533
Fax (416) 972-0533
www.ainsleyhouse.com
Credit MC, V, Interac. Enjoy this grand Rosedale mansion, in one of Toronto's most impressive neighbourhoods. The Hannigan family lives in and runs this B&B, but their living areas are off limits. City centre easily accessible.

FOURTH STREET BED & BREAKFAST

10 and 22 Fourth Street, Toronto Islands
Tel (416) 203-7551
Credit cards not accepted. Do like Torontonians do, and enjoy the peacefulness of the islands while looking out at the city's impressive skyline, just 10 minutes away. You will need to factor in the Ward's Island ferry schedule (www.toronto.ca/parks/island/summerschedule.htm). This is a privately owned B&B, so you can take the time to get to know your hosts and ask for hot tips on island life and Toronto attractions. Bicycles are included in the rates. Garden and internet available.

VICTORIA'S MANSION GUEST HOUSE

68 Gloucester Street
Tel (416) 921-4625
Fax (416) 944-1092
www.victoriasmansion.com
Credit MC, V, Interac. No breakfast provided. In the heart of the Village (Church Street), this is an option for different accommodation. It is located in an 1890s Victorian mansion, with its own peaceful garden. Look out for China, the friendly live-in gray cat! Rooms with microwaves and fridges.

ALICE FAZOOLI'S ITALIAN GRILL

294 Adelaide Street West
Tel (416) 979-1910
www.alicefazoolis.com
Alice Fazooli's is located in what was once a printing plant in downtown Toronto. It is just minutes away from the Rogers Centre or the Theatre District. It's a casual place with an early-1900 saloon feel. **Main Courses** $9.95-$25.95, **Kids meals** $6.95. **Open** 11:30am-9:30pm Mon & Tues, 11:30am-10pm Wed & Thurs, 11:30am-11pm Fri & Sat, 11:30am-9:30pm Sun. **Credit** AmEx, MC, V.

CABANA

11 Polson Street
Docks Entertainment Facility
Tel (416) 469-5655
www.thedocks.com
Cabana is a great place to eat during the summer. Sit outside in the beach environment while you enjoy a light meal. The open-air concept right on the lake offers a great view of the city and the lake. **Main Courses** $7.95-$23.50, Kids meals available. **Open** 5pm-10pm Wed-Fri, 12noon-10pm, longer hours on weekends (check website for up-to-date schedule). **Closed** Mon & Tues. **Credit** AmEx, MC, V.

HORIZON'S CAFÉ

301 Front Street West
(main pod of the CN Tower)
www.cntower.ca
At 346 metres (1,136 feet) Horizon's Café offers one of the best views of the city. A great place to enjoy a light meal. **Main Courses** $11.00-$18.50. **Open** daily.

Credit AmEx, MC, V, DC.

LONE STAR TEXAS GRILL

200 Front Street West
Tel (416) 408-4064
www.lonestartexasgrill.com
Centrally located near many downtown attractions, Lone Star Texas Grill offers visitors a Western experience. Cowboy paraphernalia and Tex-Mex foods such as steak, quesadillas, tortillas and fajitas give it a unique atmosphere. **Main Courses** $8.99-$29.99. **Kids meals** $5.99-$8.99. **Open** 11:30am-10pm (closing times vary daily) Mon-Fri, 12noon-1am Sat, 12noon-10pm Sun. **Credit** AmEx, MC, V.

OLD SPAGHETTI FACTORY

54 The Esplanade
Tel (416) 864-9761
Fax (416) 864-0956
www.oldspaghettifactory.net
Located just a short walk from the St. Lawrence Market and the Lorraine Kimsa Theatre for Young People, the Old Spaghetti Factory is a convenient place to get a meal. An old warehouse, once a blacksmith shop, is home to the restaurant. It is decorated using genuine antiques, stained glass and tiffany-type lights. It is especially popular with children – as they admire the antique elevator or the 100-year old carousel, or eat in the antique streetcar within the dining room. Delicious pasta adds to the environment to make this an extremely enjoyable experience. **Main Courses** $10.59-$19.99, **Kids meals** $5.99. **Open** 11:30am-11pm Mon-Thurs, 11:30am-12midnight Fri & Sat, 11:30am-10pm Sun. **Credit** AmEx, MC, V, Interac, DC.

RAINFOREST CAFÉ

3401 Dufferin Street (in Yorkdale Shopping Centre)
Tel (416) 780-4080
Fax (416) 780-4081
www.rainforestcafe.com
This themed restaurant has animated animals (elephants, apes, snakes), live tropical fish in large aquariums, live parrots, waterfalls and special effects. The thunderstorms have actual rain and lightning! For anyone who enjoys adventure while they eat, this is the place to go. **Main Courses** $9.99-27.99, Kids meals available. **Credit** AmEx, MC, V, Interac.

WAYNE GRETZKY'S

99 Blue Jays Way
Tel (416) 979-7825 www.gretzkys.com
Hockey fan or not, this place is an impressive shrine to the world's most famous player. The restaurant is like

a museum, where Wayne Gretzky's career highlights and memorabilia are displayed. Make sure to walk around the restaurant. A great time to visit is before, during or after a Toronto Maple Leafs game! The store sells Gretzky merchandise such as shirts and caps. **Main Courses** $15.00-$25.00. **Open** 11:30am-1am Mon-Thurs, 11:30am-2am Fri & Sat, 11:30am-11pm Sun. **Credit** AmEx, MC, V.

Other eating experiences

Toronto is one of the world's gastronomic capitals, with more restaurants per head than almost any other city and a variety afforded by a truly international population. You can find anything here, from Nepalese to Argentinian, from Caribbean to Hawaiian, from Russian to Cajun. Below are a few of the best places and occasions to sample this rich gastronomic culture.

ST. LAWRENCE MARKET SNACK BARS & DELIS

95 Front Street East (in the South Market)
www.stlawrencemarket.com

Within the South Market of the St. Lawrence Market, there are several snack bars that offer anything from seafood to meats to desserts.

Buster's Sea Cove offers a variety of seafood options. Carousel Bakery, which has been featured internationally on TV and in magazines and newspapers, is the home of the "World Famous Peameal Back Bacon Sandwich". Churrasco of St. Lawrence offers chicken, grilled meats, potatoes and salads. Crepe It Up serves... what else? Crepes! Mano's Deli has hot and cold sandwiches and salads. Mustacio's is home to the Famous Veal and Eggplant Sandwich. Paddington's Pump offers another famous peameal bacon sandwich. If you're in the mood for sushi, try Quik Sushi. St. Lawrence Pizza & Ice Cream has a variety of pizza and hot pasta dishes to go as well as ice cream straight from the dairy. **Open** 8am-6pm Tues-Thurs, 8am-7pm Fri, 5am-5pm Sat. **Closed** Sun-Mon.

WINTERLICIOUS

Various locations across Toronto. For a list of participating restaurants, visit www.menupalace.com/menupalace/Winterlicious.aspx

Winterlicious is a 14-day food festival that allows you to sample the best of the city's restaurants on a budget. Over 100 Toronto restaurants participate. Restaurants offer a prix fixe promotion in which a complete meal with several courses is offered at a fixed price. **Lunch** $15.00-$20.00, **Dinner** $25.00-$35.00.

SUMMERLICIOUS

Various locations across Toronto. For a list of participating restaurants, visit www.menupalace.com/menupalace/summerlicious.aspx

Just as Winterlicious, enjoy the Summerlicious food festival through 14 days in the summer. Over 100 Toronto restaurants offer a prix fixe promotion. **Lunch** $15.00-$20.00, **Dinner** $25.00-$35.00.

TASTE OF THE DANFORTH

Danforth Avenue East (Greek Town)

Occurs every August. For information on events and restaurants, visit www.toronto.com/tasteofthe-danforth

Although primarily focused on Greek food and culture, and located in the heart of Toronto's thriving Greek community, the festival has become a city favourite, with food from many other regions. It's a feast to the senses. Enjoy your chicken souvlaki, your rebetika music and dancing, the street animation and the broken plates. Yamas!!

TORONTO EATON CENTRE

220 Yonge Street
Tel (416) 598-8560
www.torontoeatoncentre.com
A tourist destination as well, the Toronto Eaton Centre offers over 250 shops on several levels. It is located in the busy downtown area. Open daily.

T.O.'s best shopping areas

Queen's Quay Terminal Harbourfront Centre (artsy)
Queen Street West (funky)
Queen Street East (Beach)
Yonge Street (find it all!)
Vaughan Mills, in Vaughan, is a gigantic shopping mall
Bloor West Village (deluxe)
Bloor-Yorkville, one of the top 10 shopping destinations in the world, often compared to Fifth Avenue in New York, Rodeo Drive in Los Angeles and the Magnificent Mile in Chicago.

Clockwise from top-left corner:

Pages 8-9: Tommy Thompson park map courtesy Toronto and Region Conservation Authority; Islands map courtesy City of Toronto. Page 10: public domain. Page 13: all photos PFM/JJ. Pages 14-15: WikiComm; PFM/JJ; WikiComm. Page 19: all photos PFM/JJ. Pages 20-21 (attraction 1): background photo PFM/JJ. Pages 22-23: PFM/JJ. Pages 24-25 (attraction 2): PFM/JJ; time lapse photos courtesy of Sam Javanrouh; background PFM/JJ. Page 27 (attraction 3): Casa Loma cross sections courtesy of Casa Loma/Kiwanis Club Toronto (edited and modified by JJ). Page 28 (attraction 4): courtesy of www.mikesjournal.com. Page 30 (attraction 5): both photos courtesy of the Legislative Assembly of Ontario. Page 31 (attraction 5): courtesy of the Legislative Assembly of Ontario (edited by JJ); public domain. Page 32 (attraction 6): all photos PFM/JJ. Page 35 (attraction 7): WikiComm; Slawko Waschuk. Pages 36-37 (attraction 8): all photos courtesy of Royal Ontario Museum, copyright 2007. Pages 38-39 (attraction 9): panoramic photo courtesy Ontario Science Centre. Page 38 (attraction 9): PFM/JJ. Page 39 (attraction 9): PFM/JJ; PFM/JJ; courtesy Ontario Science Centre. Page 40 (attraction 10): both photos PFM/JJ. Page 40 (attraction 10): courtesy of City of Toronto/Historic Fort York, Map by Surveyor J.B. Duberger, Royal Engineers, 181b, Library and Archives Canada, NMC-23139 (modified by Kevin Hebib). Pages 42-43 (attraction 11): all photos PFM/JJ. Pages 44-45 (attraction 12): JJ archive. Pages 46-47 (attraction 13): all photos PFM/JJ. Page 48 (attraction 14): PFM/JJ. Page 49 (attraction 14): plant photo all PFM/JJ; aerial courtesy of Toronto and Region Conservation Authority. Pages 50-51 (attraction 15): all photos PFM/JJ. Pages 52-53 (attraction 16): all photos PFM/JJ. Pages 54-55 (attraction 17): PFM/JJ; PFM/JJ; public domain. Pages 56-57 (attraction 18): PFM/JJ. Page 58 (attraction 19): courtesy of Michael Shpuntov, copyright 2004. Page 59 (attraction 19): PFM/JJ; Yoho2001/Wiki GNU-FDL 1.2. Page 60-61 (attraction 20): all photos PFM/JJ. Pages 62-63 (attraction 21): all photos PFM/JJ. Page 64 (attraction 22): all photos courtesy of Toronto and Region Conservation Authority/Black Creek Pionner Village. Pages 66-67 (attraction 23): all photos PFM/JJ. Page 69 (attraction 24): public domain; Andrew Dunn (2004)/Wiki, GNU-FDl 1.2; WikiComm.